the **SOCIAL** pro

C O D E

SECRETS TO BECOMING A SUCCESSFUL
SOCIAL MEDIA MANAGER

CARRIE RODRIGUES

BEEJA
HOUSE

Contents

ACKNOWLEDGEMENT

I want to thank my wonderful parents for never imposing any restrictions as far as my professional life was concerned. Thank you for believing in me and trusting me to make the right decisions and pursue my dream of becoming an author while I was still studying.

I would like to thank all my wonderful friends in the online space who kept encouraging me to stay consistent with writing. A huge shoutout to my super talented friend Dolly Sharma who helped me design the book cover and Surabhi Aswath who pushed me on days when I doubted the fact that I could even complete this book.

Not to forget all the creators who put out content and courses that helped me learn many of the skills I built on that I've shared here.

I cannot leave out the whole reason for the birth of this book. Geetika Saigal, founder of Beeja Education has been a strong pillar of support all through my journey. I'm really grateful to you Ma'am. Becoming an author would always have remained a dream if not for you and your patient team that helped bring it to life.

INTRODUCTION

So many social media managers yet not ONE fool proof guide!

Do you know a single course or book that takes you through the journey from being nothing to the CEO of a social media marketing agency?

Well, you do now!

In this book, I'm going to answer all the questions you could possibly have about Social Media Management.

Whether you're an aspiring Social Media Manager or someone already on the quest to make it big, if you can't seem to figure out the roadmap, I've laid it all out for you right here.

No more looking for courses that hold incomplete information leaving you to figure out most of the important parts yourself. You have everything you need hereon right in your hand.

As someone who started with zero knowledge and hit an income goal of 50k right in the 2nd month and 62k in the third, I'm going to spill all the secrets.

I have started 6 Instagram accounts of my own for 2 years, with 2 successes after 4 failures. I have carefully studied all the techniques that work and highlighted those that don't as well so you can save your time by avoiding them. Many Social Media Managers who were struggling initially are now scaling their businesses with the help of these techniques.

Karishma, a Social Media Manager from Bangalore says, "I went from being completely lost to having everything laid out for me. It's all presented on a platter. There's no height you can't reach as a Social Media Manager if you implement everything in the book."

I can guarantee that if you follow everything listed step by step, you will land your first client in less than 30 days and scale to an agency in less than 6-9 months. Don't be the person who misses out on the opportunity to land clients as a result of lack of discipline. Be the kind of person that people look up to as a source of inspiration. Be that someone who shows the rest what's really possible.

Each chapter is power-packed with habits of highly effective Social Media Managers and will give you deeper insight on several topics. Not only will you master the skills required to get ahead but you'll develop a stronger mindset as well. By the end of the book, you'll be certain that it is your mindset that will set you apart from the crowd.

However, you have got to make sure to implement the tasks listed before going ahead with them. Remember, acting on what you read is the only thing that will get you ahead. Not just reading the book from cover to cover and sitting tight.

How you can make the most out of this book:

1.   Define your 'WHY'. I know you've probably heard this a million times before but have you done it? Visualize what being a successful Social Media Manager will look like for you, how it will change your life and that of your family's, how you'll never have to worry about finances again, how you'll have the freedom to work from any place in the world at any time you like, how you'll get a chance to interact with amazing business owners across the globe and be one of the major contributing factors to the success of their business.

2.   I've assigned tasks that I call *'Boulders'* to each of the chapters to help you implement all that you learn as you go along. DO NOT move to the next chapter until you're done with ALL the previous 'Boulders'.
Remember, reading does not translate to success until you utilize what you read. No matter what course you take and what book you read, you have to make sure to implement everything as you go. If you do, trust me you'll be unstoppable.

3.   EXPECT a huge transformation. Until you train your mind to realize that this book will change your life, it won't. Visualize being one of the best Social Media Managers after you're done reading and implementing

everything I say in this book. Remember that this is not just another usual book like so many others you may have read. This is THE ONE that helps you take a steep turn and lead you on the path you knew you were always destined to walk on.

4.   Keep a separate diary to record your tasks and document your journey. Write down all the struggles you face along the way and how you overcome them. Trust me, when I say that you will love going back to read it someday and perhaps even use it as content to inspire other people and sell your courses and programs through storytelling.
Documenting can take you a long way. Even if you're not much of an expressive person through writing, maybe show up on Instagram stories talking about your journey or record video diaries for yourself. It could be anything that you're comfortable with as long as you have something to look back to.

5.   Allot a fixed time every single day to read at least 5-10 pages of this book and IMPLEMENT them that day itself. The law of diminishing intent states that the more you wait on something, the less enthusiasm you then experience to go through with it. So, say you're a night person and you have 10:00-10:30 pm allotted just to read and 10:30-11:00 pm just to implement. If you're consistent with this practice, you will soon see your career bloom.

6.	Although I spoke of being a night person, I would highly recommend to set this time in the morning since you can retain the best and new ideas usually strike when you have a fresh mind. But if you're a night owl and feel like you perform better late, by all means, do what works best for you.

7.	Remove all other distractions until you're done. There's so much to take back from this book that if you start listening to podcasts and reading other non-fiction books simultaneously, you are most likely to get overwhelmed and that will prevent you from implementing and moving forward. I've made this mistake way too often. I have bought multiple courses at the same time and implemented absolutely NONE properly. But when I stuck to one and made sure to move to the next only when I managed to squeeze everything out of the previous, that's when I saw massive growth. I want the same for you.

8.	Even after following the above steps, sometimes you may still get overwhelmed and give up, but make sure to start reading all over again if you take a long break. I'm not going to start a whole motivational speech here but really, "It's okay to fail!" Remember, the ones that succeed are those that persevere.

9.	Find someone to hold you accountable. This can be a family member or friend who keeps checking on you. But the best-case scenario would be if you find someone in the field to read this book along with you so both of you can complete the 'Boulders' together.

Honestly, I've taken more courses than I can count and read innumerable books but the key to my success so far is my accountability partner and my mentor who I can share every tiny struggle with and seek solutions instead of crying or complaining about situations.

But but but…

While accountability is a great way to stay on track, sometimes you still just won't get anything done and that's a fact.

That doesn't mean accountability is not working for you. As motivated as the two of you may be in the beginning, there comes a point where both start slacking.

But here's when it's time to mix things up.

My accountability partner and I have a WhatsApp group called accountability. It's a special group even though it's just the two of us. We talk a lot in general so we thought it would be best to leave the DMs for general texts and the group for sending our checklist at the end of the day.

What we do in here is tick across the checklist and resend it to the group at the end of the day to let each other know what tasks we've successfully completed.

If there's any task that we're unable to do for more than 3 days, we get on a call to figure out how to break it down and take practical steps to complete the task at hand. For example, working out was a challenge for both of us and with our hectic schedules, none of us was able to fit it in.

So what we decided was to start with 10mins. If our body still didn't feel like moving after that and some urgent work had to be completed, then that was that. But more often than not, those 10mins would turn into a complete workout.

Another way of segregating the checklist, that helped us prioritize tasks, is labelling the importance of tasks in each area of our lives.

Our checklist is divided into
1. Fitness goals (10k steps, workout, 3L of water, etc.)
2. Personal development goals (reading 30 pages of a book daily, listening to a podcast regularly)
3.Mental health goals (meditation, journaling, expressing gratitude, affirmations, etc.)
4.Professional goals (completing client work, coordinating with team, etc.)
5. Academic goals (study for 2hours, complete notes for 1hour, etc.)

After dividing our goals into these 5 categories, we would further arrange them in order of importance and label them as A-tasks, B-tasks and C-tasks where an A-task is most important and C is least.

10.   Finally, I do need to give you a caution that this book or any other for that matter is NOT a prescription for your career or your life. It is simply a framework. You

will ultimately have to find your way by the trial and error method in many areas to figure out what works for you.

Now that you've seen how to make the most of this book, I'll catch you on the next page where we'll figure out if Social Media Management is your thing.

IS SOCIAL MEDIA MANAGEMENT FOR YOU?

Absolutely not! Run away right now before it's too late.

Oh, and just a word of caution, please excuse my sarcasm on and off in the book, haha.

Wouldn't have put in the effort to write this book if I thought that Social Media Management was a crappy field now, would I?

There is absolutely no doubt that the industry will only grow from here.

Every business is required to be online and establish its brand name to make it big. Most business owners have way too much on their plate and sooner or later consider delegating tasks like Social Media Management.

But but but…

Just because the field has scope, doesn't mean it's meant for everybody does it?

"So how do I know if it's the right fit for me Carrie?"

Glad you asked!

Not to scare you away but Social Media Management requires you to be a master of all trades. Yes, that's right, not a jack of all trades nor a master of some.

At least when starting, you aren't equipped to hire a team.

This simply means that you have to take on the role of a designer, a copywriter, a planner and be a good conversationalist as well.

Besides all of this, you'll need to be as organized as you can get.

Your room may be a mess but if your files and documents look like that too, you'll be pulling your hair out in a matter of a few weeks, trust me.

Now for the good news!

All, and I mean ALL of the skills can be mastered if you put your mind to it.

Oh, and when you do, it sure is well worth it.

BOULDER ALERT!

As your first BOULDER, I'd urge you to contemplate on a couple of questions that will help you determine whether or not this is the right field for you:

1. Do I enjoy putting out content for my page despite not earning a penny from it?

2. Am I willing to invest a good amount of time learning at least the basics of designing and copywriting?
3. Can I communicate my concerns effectively with potential clients?
4. Am I open to constantly learning about new updates that social media brings along?

When I stepped into the world of freelancing, I had no clue whether or not I was going to continue.

All I knew was I was hungry for financial freedom so I had to find a way to get it.

I do love health and fitness so I considered starting as a coach but I wasn't sure what the target audience looked like.

At the time, there weren't too many fitness coaches in the market so I didn't know if Indians would even be receptive to the idea of having a fitness coach.

Oh and also, how would I know who all want to start living a healthy lifestyle all of a sudden? Who was my target audience?

I didn't have a mentor to guide me but I did invest in a course so I asked the course creator what she thought would be a good fit for me.

She suggested starting with Social Media Management since I did love the process of content creation and had a better understanding of the target audience here.

And so it began…

I have to admit I felt the pressure of seeing so many others already established and working with clients across the globe. It was intimidating.

I mean, the reaction is rather natural, isn't it?

People had websites created and such beautiful portfolios that mine paled in comparison.

How were clients going to pick me over them?

But I decided to put all those fears behind me and start from scratch. So, I did what I had to do.

I started with what I DID know instead of worrying about how far I had to go.

I posted content every single day, engaged using strategies that I'm going to teach you in this book and showed up consistently on Instagram stories to share whatever I was learning that would come of use to my target audience.

I started from scratch and grew to 200 followers in 10 days NONE of which were friends or family. All of those people were genuinely interested in what I had to offer and share.

Turns out, the industry does need a fresh voice every now and then.

So no matter what stage you're at, right at this moment, you've got to believe that there's a place for you and the industry just won't be the same without your presence.

Now, when you start, here are the kind of services you can offer-

Technical time!
Don't worry, I won't bore you with long explanations of the kind of services you can offer because you know by now, I only like to make things as simple as possible.

There are basically three simple categories that you can divide all services into:

1. Done for you
This is the kind of service that you take care of all by yourself. The primary agenda is to save the person's time. Most business owners will hire you for these services either because they don't have the time or the patience. When selling, you need to focus on pointing out the amount of time you'll save them and the minimal effort that will be involved from their end.
Examples- Content creation, engagement.

2. Done with you
These are services that most often require your expertise on a higher level. Business owners want team members who can brainstorm with them, discuss ideas and implement them together to take the business ahead. What you're basically selling here is yourself and your skills. You have to showcase the results you've brought the clients you've worked with previously.
Examples- Strategy calls, content planning sessions, etc.

3. Do it yourself

These are generally low ticket offers that have low to zero involvement from your end. This book is one such example in my product suite. These help a lot with passive income and are mainly for clients with a lower budget. The selling point is the amount of value for such a low price. Here you have to hit the more logical side of the brain when selling. In the other two, you've got to hit the emotional side in particular.

Examples- Prompts for Video Instagram Stories (in which the clients show up themselves).

Now you know the three kinds of services you can start offering.

I'll see you on the next page where we'll discuss the right headspace you need to be in before you even start so as to guarantee success when you eventually do begin.

RIGHT MINDSET TO BE A SUCCESSFUL SOCIAL MEDIA MANAGER

"The online space is saturated already, Carrie. I don't think there's space for me."

"I don't have any experience nor a degree. I don't think anyone will hire me."

These are just two of the million objections I've ever heard. One thing I can tell you for sure is, none of these is true, nor are any of the mind blocks that are preventing you from starting or signing good clients.

In the book '80% Mindset 20% Skills by Dev Gadhvi', I realized that for social media managers to be successful, we first need to have the mindset of one.

When I started out, I had no idea what this looked like. What should I have believed that would help me grow faster?

I read all mindset shift books and watched a tonne of general YouTube videos but the best learnings, without a doubt, were from observing other social media managers in the field. I realized many had the essential skills but what separated the successful from those that were struggling was the right mindset.

So I started watching all the possible interviews by those that were successful and started keeping note of what their unique beliefs were.

I know I may seem like a stalker to you but don't judge me, okay? Being a keen observer is one of my traits that's going to allow me to help you better through this book, haha.

Let us now take a look at some mindset shifts:

There is more than enough space for you.
When I entered the business world, I was terrified of all the competition there is in the market.

For real! I'd just type 'Social Media Manager' on Instagram and have tons of names show up.

I would then go and check out their pages and "Whoa!!" seemed like they were doing so well already.

"Why would anyone want to work with me when there are so many others with more experience?" was the thought that kept bothering me.

Every time I saw the testimonial of a successful Social Media Manager, I'd think to myself "There are a lot less clients left in the market now. I've missed the train."

Do you ever feel anything alike?

Do you ever wonder if there really is space for yet another social media manager?

Well, I'm here writing this book obviously because THERE AREN'T ENOUGH!!

The online space is only growing. Every single day there are new businesses coming up that need experts to help out with their social media.

Yes, most business owners can handle their accounts initially but when they don't see results or can no longer find the time, they realize the importance of hiring someone who can work with the right strategies. And if you stick with me to the end of this book, that person to help them is soon going to be YOU.

So get rid of the scarcity mindset. It's the season of abundance!

You aren't competing with anyone.
Even if you're charging the same as someone else, don't ever see them as your competition. Your ideal client will have a unique set of values and a style that aligns with you. If it aligns with another Social Media Manager, wish them well because this would simply mean that you now aren't wasting your time with the wrong client.

Think of it just like in marriage. If your best friend is getting married to someone great, you're nothing but happy, right? That person makes HER/HIM happy. That doesn't mean he/she would have made YOU happy too.

Soulmates and clients are just the same. So that's the end of competition in your life. From now on, no competitors, only allies.

You will never know it all nor will you ever be perfect. To date, I know there are some areas that I need to work on and learn more about. Designing on photoshop is not my strong suit. But that has never stopped me from getting ahead. When I started, I barely knew designing on Canva or even the concept of content pillars for that matter.

Yet I set out to look for clients confident that whatever their needs may be, if I wasn't equipped to assist them with it right away, it would be perfectly alright to say "I'll figure it out and get back to you by the end of the week."

The same goes for you. Always remember the motto, 'Done over perfect and progress over perfection.'

Pick the right mentor.
Don't even consider walking this path alone. No matter how much a coach costs, if you decide to invest in one, you will make back the money in no time. But if you start out trying to figure it all out on your own, it will take you months, perhaps even a year to learn everything needed and you will then have to make your own mistakes.

The right coach will prevent you from making all the mistakes they made along the way. This will speed up your journey in ways you can't even imagine.

When starting, I didn't have a role model to whom I could reach out. I was so lost as to where I could find the right coach to help me along my journey. I joined HustlePost Academy by Saloni Srivastava but still wasn't satisfied mainly because there were a lot of group sessions but not many one-on-ones. None with Saloni at least. Thankfully in 2 months, I was allotted a mentor who I cannot thank enough to this day. Shoutout to my first and best mentor Roshni Sammohi. I owe you big time!

I learnt secrets of discovery calls, packaging my services well, setting up systems, etc. all through her. We had meetings even at 6 AM sometimes. That's how dedicated she was to helping me grow.

I sincerely hope you find an amazing mentor that you resonate with too!

Have an investment mindset.
If you enter the game scared to spend money, you will automatically attract low ticket clients who are also scared to spend on you.

Invest in the right courses that you think will help upskill. Don't get me wrong, I'm all for squeezing the most out of free resources. There are some really great YouTube video series that teach a lot of important skills. That's how I started out. But in the long run, you will have to invest in high-level courses, equipment when necessary, better mentors, etc.

I had a very close friend who started freelancing way before me. She is a very responsible person whom I admire to this day but she was dependent solely on free resources and as a result that prevented her from achieving massive success. I was able to get ahead of her in 2 months only because I invested and learnt in a span of a week what can take years to pick up from individual YouTube videos.

To this day, I make it a point to reinvest at least 20% of my earnings back into my business. I don't need too much equipment so all I have bought myself so far is a laptop. Other than that, it's been mentors and courses. In fact, just yesterday I bought a new course that's teaching me so much. Definitely going to include some of my takeaways later in the book.

Implement before you buy a new course.
After I made my first investment, I was already so excited about the second that I made the purchase without even properly going through the first. This led to a sense of overwhelm. I reached a point where it started becoming more of an obsession to accumulate courses. That's when I stopped and decided on a rule.

I do not buy a new course unless I've watched AND IMPLEMENTED the old one. As simple as that!

This kind of reward system, to gift myself a new one every time I finish the last one I bought, pushes me to consume my courses quicker and see results through implementation while also keeping me excited about the next course I'm going to buy.

You don't have to charge peanuts just cause your competition is.
Can you imagine how ridiculous it would sound if Nike's owner suddenly came out and announced a drop in prices just because they heard of the rates of shoes in the market?

Crazy, isn't it? Yet why do we keep comparing ourselves to other service providers who don't have premium offers?

It's simple, most clients would rather pay 600 dollars for work well done rather than 150 dollars for someone who will keep messing up and waste their time having to micromanage everything.

Now, if you've been charging less cause you yourself don't have much to offer, those days are over!

After this book, with all the knowledge you carry, you will be the most sought Social Media Manager. Believe it and we'll achieve it together.

You deserve all the money you charge.
After you overcome the need to charge less and finally charge your time's worth, the battle isn't over. You then need to start believing that you actually deserve it. If you don't, you will soon start to see yourself adopt self-sabotaging habits that will lead you back to square one or perhaps even take you a few steps behind into the negative.

You cannot afford to repel your blessings!

To ensure you don't, make it a point to practice the affirmations listed below daily:

1. I deserve abundant wealth.
2. I deserve the best clients.
3. I deserve clients who treat me with respect.
4. I am proud of myself for working hard enough to land these clients.
5. I work with few but quality, high ticket clients.
6. Anyone who works with me is really fortunate.

Choose to be satisfied at the end of the day.
As a Social Media Manager, sometimes even after a highly productive day, we end up feeling like we still didn't really manage to do everything we'd like to have finished.

This feeling will never go away because of the amount of work that goes into Social Media Management. So the best way forward is for us to tame it.
Write down a gratitude list of things that you're glad you got done and make a conscious decision to be happy about how you spent your time through the day and applaud yourself for the amount you DID get done instead of beating yourself up about what you didn't.

Something that can possibly help you get more efficient along with time is to list one thing you could have done differently that day. In doing so, the next time a similar situation arises, you will be more inclined to tackle it well.

Additionally, sometimes during this exercise, you'll realize that some of the things you beat yourself up about are actually the best way forward. There's no better way you'd rather have it done.

For example, I'd always get upset that I wasn't able to get my workout in during my evenings. But when I sat down to write what I can do to change it, I realized that there are client meetings and coaching calls that are inevitable. I couldn't possibly manage to get a workout done before 7:30 and then I have family prayers at 8. Half an hour isn't enough to workout and shower. So the easiest way forward was moving my workout session to mornings. There on, my guilt of not being able to workout in the evenings went out the door.

We have to accept that we probably aren't going to be able to complete everything we would ideally like to do in a day. But we've done more than enough, so how about we shift the focus to that, give ourselves a pat on the back and find something that gives us joy at the end of the day and helps us unwind?

Believe you can find a blue ocean within the red.
I once attended a live webinar where I heard a very interesting concept that has helped me in many areas of my life. This is the concept of finding a blue ocean.

Now, we've all heard of the phrase, 'There are many fish in the sea', right? All of these fish are most often swimming in what's called the red ocean, a place where there's a lot of competition, a lot of backstabbing, a lot of betrayals and a lot of slaughtering of each other's dreams in order to get to the top. This is a place where there's a lot of competition that is unhealthy. So in order to escape this and still succeed, the best way forward is to find what the speaker in that session referred to as a blue ocean.

 Now, a blue ocean is essentially a place that not many other people have discovered, or you have come up with it yourself. It's a space where there is an ample amount of place for your dreams to flourish without worrying about anybody else competing for your place.

I'm sure you're wondering how you can get to this place, right?

The better question though is how will you create this blue ocean for yourself?

All you have to do is come up with an idea that not many other people have thought of or have been working on. Now, this concept doesn't really fit in with the field of social media management. I mean, we all know how much competition there is.

So for a very long time, this is what held me back from starting. I kept wondering if the competition would get to me. Was it a smart move to make by getting into a field where there is already so much competition?

However, I realized eventually that it is possible to find your own blue ocean within a red ocean. And so what I did was I found a unique selling proposition (USP) for myself, which helped me stand out from the rest of the

Social Media Managers and helped me create my own little blue pool.

In my blue pool, I was swimming almost alone by posting stories consistently by showing up and offering my viewpoints, sharing what I knew about social media, being confident no matter what, setting boundaries with clients, implementing everything that I could and so on and so forth.

There were hardly any other Social Media Managers who were following through with all of that had to be done to get ahead. And so I managed to find my own place in this big red ocean. Why am I choosing to mention this in this book? Mainly because a lot of people have the same mindset.

A lot of us tend to hide behind the competition, fearing that we won't be able to compete or that we won't be good enough. But here's a message that no matter who you are or where you're from, if you implement every single thing in this book, I can guarantee that you will find your own blue ocean that you can swim happily in and you will never feel the need to compete with anybody else in your industry. So read on.

Start FEELING the progress.
The only thing more important than making progress is FEELING it.

First, you've got to define what progress means to you. Is it the money that you're after (which isn't a bad thing at all like society gets us to believe at times) or is it the freedom?

Each of us has a deep-rooted inner desire that we've got to figure out and satisfy accordingly. That's the only way to really feel progress.

Once you start to feel like you're moving forward, you work even harder to go further. It's just how it is. Take the example of gymming. When you go to the gym for the first few weeks and barely see any results, it starts feeling so pointless and you almost want to quit.

But when you see those gains or the weight starts shedding off, it starts getting exciting and slowly addictive.

When it comes to Social Media Management or just freelancing in general, it's very important to fall in love with the process. I'm not saying every aspect of it but at least most of what you do on a daily basis.

To make this happen, the best way is to start tracking progress. Write down your income goals and make sure you're setting targets and celebrating your wins both big and small.

When you're able to go out or take your family out for a meal and not look at the prices of the food cause you finally have financial stability, when you're able to take off days without feeling guilty, when you can pick your work timings, all these are small signs of progress and the fact that you can actually work on your terms which were rather one of your main reason to start this side hustle.

I know all of this may seem like a lot but to help fix it in, here's your next simple BOULDER:

Pick each of these points and journal on anyone per day. Figure out how you can rewire your brain to truly believe each. Be as specific as possible!

See you on the next page where you'll learn how you can be your most confident self, a trait that's super important as a social media manager both when you have to show up online and on discovery calls as well.

SHOWING UP WITH CONFIDENCE

Confidence and I go a long way and trust me, I know it's the biggest secret!

Are you ready for it? I know you won't believe me but here goes anyway…

Confidence doesn't care if you make sense or not.

Yup, that's right. It really doesn't.

As shameful as this may sound, I have to admit that I attribute most of my accolades to my confident demeanour. Back in school, I could beat most of the public speaking competitors not because I had the smartest thing to say but because I sounded convincing. I can guarantee that if you take a look at the scoreboard, it would be the marks for delivery that got me those wins.

When I started my Instagram page, I got myself to believe that my journey was just like Jennifer Anniston . I showed up as if people couldn't wait to hear my point of view and rightly, I attracted EXACTLY that!

By showing up on stories believing I was an expert (even when I had no first-hand experience whatsoever), I was able to grow my following and make some really amazing friends who are really close to my heart to this day.

Had I kept overthinking and wondering what people around me would think of me, I would never ever have been here today.

No matter what your niche is, if you show up as an expert and confidently state your opinion, people are definitely going to be drawn to you and treat you with respect.

Starting my 1:1 consultation calls when I myself had been in the industry for only three and a half months was really intimidating. After a couple of people booked my calls, knowing that they had even more experience than me scared the living hell out of me.

But nonetheless, I showed up on those calls with confidence believing there was something I learnt along my journey that would come of use to them and sure enough, it did. Ask any of my mentees and they will willingly tell you how much value they took back from my calls.

No matter who you get on your next discovery call with, no matter how much experience they have and how old they are, show up on the call believing you know at least a little more than them (about social media if nothing else).

Let me tell you about Shruti, my first close friend in the online space. She was 17 when I met her. I was honestly mind blown when she told me her age. If you saw her show up In instagram stories, you could never have guessed she was that young.

She showed up every single day to talk about her offers, her unique strategies, her journey, her struggles and in every story she posted, all you could see was confidence in who she was and what she could bring to the table.

She wasn't easily intimidated by her clients who were more than double her age, she was unafraid to offer advice to people even triple her age. She once even told me about an accomplished 65 year old she was working with and how much he valued her work.

If she allowed the number on her birth certificate to determine her worth, she wouldn't have hit her six-figure goal even to this day.

A lot of us shy away because of our background, language, our looks, our age, etc. when in fact the only ones judging you for all those factors are YOU and those useless internet trolls who have never and will never do anything useful with their life either way.

Present yourself as someone who knows what they're doing. When they see that you know your way around, they are highly likely to entrust their business to you.

But go the other way round, no matter how good your skillset is, if you aren't confident about what you bring to the table, you can kiss clients goodbye.

Another thing to keep in mind and this one's sort of a reality check…

NOBODY CARES ABOUT YOU!

I know it sounds a little demeaning but isn't it really an advantage? This is THE BEST TIME to make mistakes without the whole world seeing or hearing about them.

I mean think about it, if Jennifer Aniston posted a horrible quality image/video, there will be a million articles questioning and ridiculing it. Who knows how many memes!

But you don't have to worry about that right now so go try new things, test the waters, experiment with that idea at the back of your mind. In everything you do, carry confidence in your front pocket.

Now that being said, I'm sure you'll come back asking for practical steps to take that will help boost confidence.

So, guess what? I'm going to reveal all the secret steps that I only ever tell my high paying 1:1 consultation clients.

Are you ready?

BOULDER:
1. Just pick up your phone or any device with a camera and record yourself.
2. Watch the video, keep rewatching and takedown pointers you think you can improve on. (Remember not to dwell on how bad you may look right now. Just

remind yourself that it will be a good transformation video to show your 'before' someday when you are confidently speaking in front of a huge audience.)

3. Now, start working on each thing you've pointed out. (Be it hand movements, eye contact, pronunciations, etc.)
4. Record yourself again keeping everything in mind.
5. Watch the recording with all the pointers ahead of you and strike out whatever you've managed to improve on.
6. Record again now keeping whatever is left in mind and then show a close friend or family member who can give constructive criticism.
7. Note down whatever they say and record yourself again after working on their pointers.
8. Show it to them and if they see improvement, there you go! You're ready to shoot stories and reels confidently now AND show up on discovery calls too.

PRO TIP: Even after completing the steps, if you still aren't confident enough, start by posting stories only for close friends. Add people you're comfortable with even if it's just 5 people.

Start here and slowly with time, you can transition to posting for all.

When you're done completing this BOULDER or any other for that matter, don't forget to share it on your Instagram stories and tag me @carrie.deanna . I'd love to cheer you on and help you in any way possible to get better and more confident.

You got this! I believe in you more than anyone else ever will. The very fact that you're reading this, shows that not only do you want to get better but you're also actively looking out for ways to learn how to and that in itself is a HUGE step.

On the next page, let's discuss how you can show up confidently consistently by managing your time well.

How To Manage Time As A Social Media Manager

We all know that one person who ALWAYS claims to be busy but never really accomplishes anything extraordinary, right?

When I was young, I'd always assume people on calls during parties were very important, highly accomplished people.

But as I grew up I realized that's far from the truth. The only thing you can say about them is the fact that they have their priorities messed up.

Parties are a time to bond with friends and family. If someone doesn't have the time for that, they are obviously too consumed by their work, which trust me, isn't a good sign at all.

With the right systems, you can find a way to be

productive in short intervals so you never find yourself too busy to follow through with activities that truly matter whether it is playing badminton with your little brother or helping your mum with cooking.

So here are some time management hacks that I hope will help speed things up and make you more efficient as a Social Media Manager.

When on social media, it's easy to lose track of time. We start scrolling through reels and before you know it, you spend 3 hours on 'market research.'

Today, I won't tell you most of the common hacks. You can get loads of free content all over the place.

So let's focus on tasks that we can actually implement.

At the end of this chapter, I share a couple of extra time management tricks only for social media managers.

BOULDER 1:

Step 1: Make a list of things you CANNOT afford to miss the next day. Label them as A tasks

Step 2: Then write down the things you would like to get done and label them as B, C, etc. in the order of priority.

Step 3: Write down all the hurdles you think you will face during the day.

Step 4: Plan all the ways you can overcome these hurdles.

Done with the planning!

Now, let's be honest, we have all tried to maintain timetables. For some of us, it works well, but this is for all of you who can't keep up with it.

The Scoreboard Principle states that anything you track, you do better at.

So if being time-bound doesn't work for you, we have got to find another way of tracking, right?

Let's try something I call reverse listing. Here, we will list out what we do only when we're done doing it instead of planning the day down to every minute beforehand and getting upset when we can't stick to it.

BOULDER 2:
Maintain a separate diary altogether on which you write down every task AFTER you've completed it. This gives you a dopamine release after each task thus motivating you to complete the next task soon.

Note that the order of completing tasks should preferably be in alphabetical order as discussed in BOULDER 1.

Special hacks for Social Media Managers to save time:

1.   Schedule posts on Creator Studio or Planoly.

DO NOT skip this! I ignored the scheduling for so long. I just felt why not post daily? It's not like I don't have a few minutes to spare every evening. But firstly, these few moments here and there add up and it can really start to get to you. Secondly, having to find the creative and caption even if you've organized it well does take up quite a bit of time. Thirdly, you can hang out with friends, go for a walk in the evening or watch a movie with the family. Basically, scheduling gives you the freedom and relieves you of the constant stress of forgetting to post at the time your clients/ your own audience is most active.

2.   Allot a set time each day to each client and stick to the same timing every day.

If you're starting out, you may not see the importance of this yet. But eventually, when you grow (which I'm sure will be sooner than you think), juggling between multiple clients can get really confusing. The best way to organize things is to have a set time for each of your clients and inform them about the same.

3.   Maintain a list of questions you need to ask a particular client and go to them after you have at least five questions, instead of frequently bothering them to ask one at a time. This will save more time than you think.

How often have you gone time and again asking one question after the other?

Well if you haven't, you can just skip this part cause I'm about to embarrass myself and tell you that I've asked clients more than 18 questions at different points on THE SAME DAY!!!

Don't judge me okay?

4. Batch similar tasks. Since your brain is already used to the task, it goes faster instead of having to retrain your brain each time you switch to a new task.

   Example- Creating 5 posts at a time will take way less time than 1 post per day for 5 days.
   Creating the invoices for all your clients at the same time is also super quick. When you sit down to research for a client, do it for all other clients at that time too.

5. Break tasks down into steps so that it goes way faster and you're less likely to procrastinate.

   Example: Instead of saying post for a client tomorrow. Break it down into creating a graphic, writing a caption, getting hashtags ready, setting an alarm or scheduling to post at the clients optimal time.

   When there's a huge task ahead of us, we tend to push it further and further away out of fear but when you have small easy tasks, you're more likely to get ahead.

HOW TO UPSKILL THE RIGHT WAY

In my initial days, no wait, who am I kidding?

Until four months back, I kept learning things from random places. One minute I was watching a video on brand strategy, the next minute on launching a new program.

I knew where I wanted to land eventually so I was trying to learn everything that would get me there. I absolutely love courses so I bought one after the other. There was HustlePost Academy by Saloni Srivastava first then some Udemy courses, Marketing Accelerator By Roota Mittal, launching black Friday sale by Sonitha Mandava and the list is endless.

In doing all of this, I ended up learning bits of everything but what I lacked was a clear roadmap.

I wanted a step by step approach to get where I wanted to go. I mean think about it, we all like it handed over to us, right? A systematic guide as to how to go from point A to point B. When we want our driver's licence, we join a driving school or ask someone we trust to teach us, when we want to learn to cook, we take a cooking class or learn from our parents perhaps. For most areas of our life, we know the basic steps. Yet there aren't enough people talking about the step by step plan to becoming a confident six-figure business owner who's leaving an impact.

So, here I am sharing the exact step by step approach you need to take while learning how to structure your time set aside to upskill.

BOULDER

1. Figure out your end destination eg: Own my own Digital Marketing Agency
2. Break it down into a step by step path to get there. Eg: First sign high ticket clients, then hire a team to delegate tasks that drain me, then focus on upskilling and get even more and better clients.
3. Set deadlines for each of the steps Eg: Get my first client in 30 days, next 3-5 in two months, then hire 6 months down the line.
4. Break it down further into actionable steps you need to take daily to get there and all that you need to learn for the same. Eg: The client acquisition techniques you plan on using.
5. Start a course/ Read a book that talks about this in particular and devote your whole 1hr of upskilling in a day solely to this. I'd recommend purchasing courses when you're at a stage where you can afford them.

Most free courses lack depth and random YouTube videos lack structure. Investing your money also ensures that you are more invested in. devoting your time to the process of learning. I mean think about it, if you start a free course and take a break from it, you're unlikely to come back to it most often because you have nothing to lose but when you invest your money, it's a waste unless you watch and implement which will push you to take it more seriously.

Caution: When you're on the lookout for courses that align with your goal, you will be allured to several other programs which may be great but if they don't lead you to the destination you have in mind, you will have to say a straight NO!

Respect the phase of your life that you're currently in.

Another thing to keep in mind is to go into each new course with the belief that you will implement it and it's going to upgrade your life to a whole new level. Truly believe it and it is bound to happen.

SHOULD YOU CREATE A NEW INSTAGRAM HANDLE FOR YOUR BUSINESS?

How many do you have right now? I'm guessing one basic with family and friends…or maybe not family, haha!

When starting out, I wish someone had told me a clear answer as to whether or not I should create a new account or stick with my old ones.

Being someone who had already created FIVE Instagram accounts for different purposes, I was skeptical about whether or not a new one would really do much good. Oh and yes, you read it right, I really did have 5 accounts.

Previously, I had one account for my art. I used to regularly post all the kinds of drawings that I used to do, all the paintings and so on and so forth so that I could sell a few here and there and make some money and use it as a side hustle. But when this didn't kick off in the way that I hoped, my hopes sank and I started doubting myself.

That was when my interests changed, and I started with a fitness page. On this page, I would post regularly about the health benefits of working out and living a healthy lifestyle and all the different kinds of things that I would learn to do with health and wellness. But eventually, I realized that this page wasn't growing either.

I got really frustrated at the fact that I was putting in so much effort and I didn't see any results that I hoped I would. So I wasn't confident that I could be a Social Media Manager and really help other people across the globe to come up with content that would really do well and this was what made me doubt myself. But when I started my own account, especially for social media management, I decided that I wouldn't invite any friends or family, and I would focus mainly on getting a new audience.

This was one of the best decisions I could make because I did not tell a single person in my friend circle that I had started this account, and as a result, the people who are following me are all people who are relevant to my target audience. Either they're people in the same industry, which is other social media managers or they're potential clients like coaches, authors and so on.

In the beginning, since I hadn't figured out who my target audience was, I started following everybody whether it was product-based or service-based businesses. And if you are setting up, I would recommend the same until you niche down.

What this does is, it basically trains the algorithm who else to show your posts to. In this way, your content will appear to exactly the right people who you intend to target. These will be people who will potentially buy from you in the future. They will either turn into clients or they will turn into mentees in the future if you start with one-to-one consultation or any kind of course.

Personally, why I decided to interact with other Social Media Managers is because I knew that in the long run I was looking to coach. To this date, I interact with a lot of other Virtual Assistants and Copywriters as well who are within the similar niche so that I can help them either via DMs or the offers that I launch.

I know that it may seem scary. It does seem daunting in the beginning to start off with zero followers, especially the first day when you initially create your account. I can still remember that time. I did not know whom to ask to follow me nor who all to approach.

I mean, think about it. Who would follow someone who has zero followers? Why would they follow them?

So I moved to the second question. I asked myself why I wanted people to follow me, and that was when I realized that I wanted to be seen as an expert.

So before I went out and engaged with other people, I first made sure to create valuable content on my page. I put out two posts the first day itself and made sure to be active in my stories and have my highlights updated. I created an about me highlight. I created it and a highlight for my services in particular, and I created a highlight for mini-training, and I would recommend you to do the same. At least three highlights should be in place in the beginning.

Then what I started doing was I started showing up on Instagram stories. Once these were in place, I decided to go about and start engaging. The minute I started engaging and people came back to my page and saw value, they followed back eventually. This was what helped me grow to 200 followers within ten days, right from zero, none of which were friends and family (To stress on that again).

"Impressive!" You would say. Well, I wouldn't.
With the right strategy, you can do the same, if not better. I can assure you that if you start out from scratch and target only the people that you have in mind and you eventually see yourself working with you will grow to endless bounds.

Yeah Carrie, easy to say but how do I even start from scratch? Who do I get to follow me?

Chances are you barely know anyone who's your target audience and that's PERFECTLY fine.

Too many people are focused on gaining followers instead of first providing value.

Why would some stranger from the other end of the world follow you if they aren't getting something from your content?

You've got to give them value through your posts.

Now, another thing to keep in mind is not to just post introductions of yourself and your brand. By all means, create an introductory post but there also has to be some valuable/ relatable/ fun content.

At the end of the day, people only care about what's in it for them and your role is to point that out.

Here's what you need to make sure you do in the beginning:
1. Optimize your bio.
2. Logo/good quality profile picture.
3. Highlights section intact.
4. At least 3 posts of value.

Once you look at your feed and you're satisfied with it yourself, you can then show up with confidence and reach out to people without feeling as insecure as you did before.

Now I'm sure your next question is whom to reach out to right?
See? I read minds haha. I got you.

You need to reach out to exactly the people that you're targeting in your bio. If it's product-based businesses you want to start with, then look for toy shops, oat milk companies, tea brands, tile companies, sweet shops, etc. If you're inclined towards helping service-based businesses then interact with mindset coaches, fitness instructors and/or teachers.

You've got to check out their content and offer genuine compliments. Then start building a conversation, give them a free audit perhaps and invite them on a zoom call. You can casually put it as "Let's have a coffee chat!"

Over the call, understand what stage they're in right now with their business. If you think you can fit in and help them grow, pitch your services with a one-time offer price. There you go!

Now, don't be discouraged if your first few don't convert. Keep getting on calls, analyzing what went wrong and trying to pitch better with each call. Eventually, sales will be a piece of cake to you and you will then be unstoppable.

My journey to my first paid offer on Instagram.
My first experience of being placed with a paid opportunity on Instagram was rather strange. I started a

faith account where I'd share my daily testimonies of how God was working in my life.

I adopted the Follow-Unfollow method. Spent hours on it actually. Gosh! The amount of time I wasted.

But in a couple of weeks, I started getting DMs. Since we were under lockdown at the time, I didn't have much else to do so I'd spend hours on the account having conversations with people.

There was this one person in particular who kept sending texts. He seemed decent so I did respond in the beginning but it was far too often that he would send in a text and since I was interacting with so many new people daily, I often would forget to reply to the old ones.

Somehow he persisted and one day he wrote me a poem that was really kind. After that, we started having more conversations and all of a sudden one day he went "Would you like to teach math to a bunch of students in the UK?"

At first, I thought it was some kind of charity and since I didn't have much to do anyway, I obliged.

Only later when we began to discuss the details did he ask me if 500INR per lesson was a good deal.

After struggling to get students for even 100INR per hour in India, this seemed like it was too good to be true. I still remember the day I went and stood in a line at the Western

Union to collect my first pay. It was just 2000INR but it was the first of my earnings so it meant a lot. That day when I held the envelope with money in my hands is when I began to realize that the possibilities In the online space are limitless.

I taught math for about 3 weeks and when they liked my style of teaching, I was able to pitch other lessons like public speaking, verbal and non-verbal reasoning, piano, crochet, mandala art, etc.

Every single penny I earned, I saved so I could invest in something that would help me get better.
Yes, I did gift my family things, buy a few food items here and there but I tried to save as much as I could.

After a few months, I was approached by a network marketing company and had to invest 30,000 INR. Everyone in my family was against it but thankfully since I had the money saved, I didn't need much. Whatever little, I borrowed from my close friends. 1,000-2,000INR each and returned it in a few weeks.

That was my first step into marketing. I learnt lead generation, cold calling, follow-ups and so much more from them.

I don't regret a single moment but after some point, I realized that there was only so much I could grow there. I wanted more. I was hungry to be independent, be my own boss.

There, I still felt very dependent. I had to bank on the system, my upline (people connected above me) and I started feeling like someone very desperate. I didn't like the side it was bringing out of me.
So I quit. I made 40k so I ensured there was no loss and then decided to look for better.

That's when I came across Saloni's YouTube video that introduced me to the world of freelancing and showed me one path there that was HustlePost Academy.

It was almost 8,000 INR at the time. Seemed like a pretty big amount to invest in a course so I took my time doing some research, asking around, approaching as many people as I could looking for feedback.

After about 2 months I suddenly woke up one day and decided I couldn't wait anymore. There was this whole new life calling me and I had to pay heed. So I opened the site and made the payment!
Only later in the day did I realize I had my exams a week later. Ugh! Talk about bad timing.

I didn't really care though. Exams were online. I knew I'd somehow clear them. So I began binge-watching the modules one after the other taking notes of every little new thing I picked up. I went over the notes time and again until I knew for sure that I could retain everything. Yeah, I know, total nerd!

Now, many people will disagree with this method. I know

it sounds crazy but I thought at the time that this would work better for me. I watched all the modules and only then did I make the decision to take up Social Media Management.

Most experts advise to watch and implement as you go. That's some very sane advice and I recommend the same for you when reading this book or any other.
I admit I made a mistake and the only reason I'm sharing it is to prevent you from making the same.

When you learn too many new things at once it can lead to overwhelm and you don't end up really implementing any of it properly. If not for the peer mentorship program that was part of the academy I enrolled in, I don't think I'd have implemented any of the things I had learned honestly.

My mentor helped me break down everything so well that I didn't once feel overwhelmed in the process. I could take one step at a time and land my first client after putting in consistent effort. Of course, since we were under lockdown, I had no other commitments either so I could afford to invest all my time into building my side hustle which isn't always a luxury for everyone at all times but in any case, I'd say always set a timeline for yourself and make sure it's realistic according to your schedule.

So yes, this is the story of how I started out. You'll hear more stories and experiences all through the book.

I've sprinkled them in just to make the read more interesting so you find things you can relate to. I hope you start to realize that I am just as ordinary as you and if I could turn things around, so can you.

Niche down

We have all at some point wondered whether this is a good idea right? Would it be better to narrow down which industries you'd like to work with?

If you're just being introduced to Social Media Management, then probably not. But sooner or later you will definitely be asking yourself what niche you love working on most.

Now, in my opinion, deciding to niche down has its own pros and cons. I wouldn't like to take sides because while I haven't yet niched down, I do have a particular industry in mind that I'd like to serve so fingers crossed, I might be making the switch soon. But this is for you if you're in two minds and can't figure out if you ought to niche down or not.

Pros:

1. Helps you use your learnings in one client account to benefit the other.
2. Content pillars and strategy will be very similar so less work goes into it.
3. You can invest your time into learning about the field knowing it will definitely come to great use since each client will benefit from it.
4. People within the niche will be more inclined to work

with you compared to a general SMM.

Cons:
1. Limits your options and if you niche down to service-based, it puts off product-based business owners when they visit your page.
2. Research process tends to get boring since you're reading so much about one topic itself.
3. You can't repeat topics in two clients accounts so that requires a lot of variety of content in the long run.

Now the decision lies in your hands. Even when something has more pros than cons, it isn't necessarily the right step for you since the cons may be way more intense.

Product based vs service based.
If you're thinking of niching down, this chapter is specially for you to decide whether to opt for product based or service-based.

Creating content to ask people to buy a tangible product vs getting people to invest in themselves has entirely different requirements.

At the end of the day sure you need to create posts, stories and add hashtags but the thought process differs.

How? Well for one, product-based businesses generally don't need long captions. You simply state the specifications that are given to you by the business owner and here and there maybe add a few witty lines.

But for service-based like a health coach/life coach/mindset coach, you need to dive deep and create problem awareness content that involves long creative captions.

So if you're someone who loves writing, service-based will probably be a better fit but if writing is the part you dread most about being a social media manager or if you think it takes up too much time and brain space, product-based is the way to go.

In order to simplify the decision-making process for you, I've laid out a couple of pointers to reflect on:

1. Less freedom with pictures for product-based since they are generally provided to you. There's only so much you can do when you're bound to share only what's given rather than be able to look for your own stock images. This can prove to be a good thing if you don't have much time to spend on designing but isn't so much fun when you're a creative person.

2: Sometimes big product based companies require heavy designing skills and the use of software like photoshop that will probably force you to hire someone if you don't have the skills. This will cut down on your income.

3: Success will be measured on the number of sales for product-based so there's more responsibility for you and hardly any for the client while service-based requires the client to be actively involved thus 2 minds working on the business.

However, if you like working independently and taking on the responsibility of converting leads into customers, there's nothing better than product-based.

4: If the products are delivered only to specific locations, this limits your target audience. For example- A bakery/restaurant that wants customers to visit the place. So it makes no sense to reach out to non-Goans to visit a restaurant in Goa unless of course they plan on visiting which we'll never really know.

However, this could be true even for service-based. I worked with a counselling firm that preferred their audience to be mainly from the place they were based.

Now, make sure you're geared up cause the best is on the next couple of pages!

SLAYING ON INSTAGRAM

I have started 6 Instagram accounts OF MY OWN!

Yup! I said SIX. So, this platform is very close to my heart.

I've had years of trial and error and hence want to help you avoid all that and set you up for success right now.

There are a number of things to keep in mind. It may be overwhelming so make sure to highlight things and keep coming back to revise.

Optimize your profile

It's everywhere!

All business coaches are constantly giving out this advice and that's only because it really is super important. Only once your profile is optimised will people be able to easily find you and soon then hire you.

But what does that really mean?
What are the steps you can take to make sure your profile is optimized?
Well, it's way simpler than you think, trust me. I spent weeks trying to find out what this 'optimization' is. I read books, took courses, spoke to the experts and ultimately realized, it's actually pretty simple.

So here's my attempt at breaking it down in the simplest possible way for you.

First, take a look at your Instagram handle.
(This is one that people use to tag you.)

Few guidelines to keep in mind:
1. Simple is best, makes it easy for people to recollect.
2. Avoid special characters and numbers. Makes it seem spammy.
3. If you aren't too creative or haven't yet niched down, having your name is best. If you have a common name like Pooja or Neha, maybe add social before it or official.

Now moving to your Instagram name.

Here it's important to keep in mind that you have to include your niche-specific words which in our case is Social Media Manager. It's best to have your name, a bar and the words Social Media Manager itself so that when business owners look for team members, your name is likely to show up.

How to optimize your bio?
1. Mission statement-
A. Who you serve(your target audience)
B. What you do
C. How you can help them
Example- I help fitness coaches build a powerful social presence with engaging content.
Who you serve-fitness coaches
What you do- build a powerful social presence
How you do it- through engaging content.

Now if you haven't picked a niche yet, that's perfectly fine. Here's an example for you: Helping you elevate your business on social media organically.

2. Previous achievements like how many clients you've worked with. This gives people reassurance.

3. Call To Action(CTA) to book a call with you or DM to work together. I personally don't like adding my calendly link because I had some random people book calls and waste my time so I prefer 'DM to know more'. It's so much better to have a conversation with a client before you send them a link to book a call. Calendly is a basic software that is free to use. It's best if you set up your account on it and have the link ready to send them any potential clients who would like to book a call after they speak to you in the DMs.

(If CTA is something you haven't heard of before, a Call to Action as the name suggests is the action you expect your audience to take when they read the sentence.)

Some examples of what NOT to include in your bio

-Age: Does it really even matter?

-Zodiac sign- Nobody cares!

- Relationship status- Married/single has nothing to do with your work.

-Dog mom-Show pictures of your dogs in your story but don't take up valuable space in your bio

-No DMs please- It will only drive people away which is exactly the opposite of your aim.

Now onto the highlights. This was something I set up before I posted anything or reached out to anyone. I didn't do it perfectly in the beginning but after learning from the experts who do it best, these are some of the highlights I'd recommend showcasing:

1. About me- Here you have a chance to talk more about yourself as a person. Your values, your 'Why' for starting this venture and anything fun your audience will benefit from knowing about you. I'd also highly recommend showcasing your systems and workflow here to give your potential clients an understanding of how you'll be working on tasks behind the scenes if they hire you. You can also create a separate highlight for this called 'Behind The Scenes or BTS'.

2. My services- What all do you offer? How many edits, how many hours do you work in a day. You can be as specific as you want here. The idea is basically to answer as many questions as you think a potential client may have about your services.

3. Testimonials- Here is your chance to show off all the previous results you've got from clients. If you don't have any, work with a few beta clients and make sure you mention 'In exchange for a testimonial' clearly before working together.

4. Mini training- This is my absolute favourite so I saved the best for the last. I have grown to this level today mainly because of mini training and engagement. So many people who I'd reach out to would follow me back even when I barely had 10 followers only because they saw the value I was putting out. They may have had thousands of followers but they knew they could learn something from me and that was incentive enough.

Share whatever you learn on a regular basis here. Be it from this book/ some course you've watched or some blog you've read. Share everything that is relevant to your niche. Remember that you don't have to hold back.

Tell your audience what you know.

Educate them with the 'what' and then they'll hire you for the 'how'.

This applies to any field but what this basically means in the field of Social Media is to tell them what they need to know inorder to build a strong social presence and they will then hire you to show them how. Tell them what all they need to do eg: optimize their bio, create a plan for their content,etc. The psychology behind this is that when it's time to actually do what you've told them, they will realise that it's better to delegate it to someone like you with expertise.

Now besides these 4, there are quite a few highlights you can come up with. Here are some fun ones:

1. FAQs- Frequently asked questions can be useful to answer to avoid answering the same doubts to potential clients individually. Some people don't even take a keen interest unless they find all the info they need about you when they visit your profile itself. So answering these questions can help retain your target audience.

2. Milestones- Taking people along with you in your journey can be a great way to build a connection and a chance to tell your brand story. Besides, highlighting small wins adds joy to your daily life. So it will end up being a good practice for you too.

3. Freebie- Using the same logic of having test drives to give the customer an unforgettable experience so that they buy the car, freebies give your audience the tip of the iceberg that you have to offer.

Whether it's some editable Canva templates or hashtag cheat sheets, people love value for free so having a highlight with all your free resources can help you reach more people. When someone downloads your free guide, likes it and shares it with their business friends, imagine the kind of exposure you'll get.

4. Collaborations- I can't number the times I've gone live. I've honestly lost count. Most of them have been conducted by the other person so there's no record on my feed. Having a separate highlight button is the only way to keep track of myself and show my audience who I've interacted with, not forgetting to mention exposing them to all the value you shared in those live sessions.

5. Consultation call details - At some point when you're confident that you're at least 5 steps ahead of some other business owners, you can launch 1:1 Consultation calls. This is an easy and fulfilling way of increasing your revenue. Having a highlight button will ensure leads flow in regularly for the same.

6. Reminders- You can post useful checklists, motivational quotes or even simple gratitude reminders or drink water reminders. This one doesn't have a strong purpose but doesn't hurt to have a highlight now, does it?

That's about it with highlights. Before we move to learn about posts, let's first understand what our aim is through our content and profile.

When your target audience lands on your page, there are 3 stages you need to take them through. Let us break each of them down now. Here's what we call the KLT factor:

1. Know(K)- First, you want our audience to be clear as to who you are and what you do.
2. Like(L)- Then comes the part where you try and get them to like you thus developing a preference over the other people in your industry.
3. Trust(T)- Here is when they see your content regularly and begin to start placing their trust in your expertise.

Now, let's understand the different kinds of posts you can create and the advantages of each.

1. Static posts: Instagram started with these. They are simple, easy to create posts that can either be just pictures or simple quotes or checklists. There are many who use them for topics like 'How to' and 'Steps to' but these aren't easy to digest so I'd say the best way to do this would be to turn it into a carousel by dividing the information. Infographics are a type of static post that is easily digestible and in my experience perform really well. These are basically pictorial representations of concepts you're trying to explain to your audience.

2. Carousel: These generate a lot of comments and saves which are really great to please the algorithm and push your post to more people. At the end of the day, our goal is to befriend the algorithm, isn't it?
    Instagram also brings up your carousel again to your audience showing them the second picture in case they didn't engage the first time. Won't you make use

of Instagrams kindness?

3. Reels: This is in my opinion the quickest way to batch create content and have it ready and organized in the drafts section of Instagram itself. While having fancy transitions are great, if you're a busy social media manager with more than 2 clients, it can get too time-consuming to explain to the client and then make the required edits. So it's best to have short reels under 7secs. The easiest is lip sync and in case of product-based businesses, videos of the products with trending audios will do the trick.

4. IGTVs- These are videos longer than 60 secs.

5. Live streams: Initially going live may seem scary but within the first few minutes, you'll start getting comfortable. The best part is you can't really see the people listening, unlike zoom.
    Make sure to save them to your feed or ask the host who invites you to share it in theirs so that those who missed it can go back and you yourself can when you grow just to see how far you've come.

6. Guest posts: These work incredibly well to grow your network and get more exposure if you provide amazing value in the post you send across to another creator to post on their feed. Note that when creating it, you need to use their brand colours.
    Creators with a similar following to you will not charge anything generally but if you go to request

bigger accounts, you have to ask them for their prices as well. It's generally around 1rupee per follower.

Okay Carrie, got it! But that still doesn't really help me with what exactly to post.

I hear you!

Once you understand this, the next step is to figure out what kind to create.

Content pillars help with exactly that. Now, I'm going to lay out **8** different types of content pillars every business owner should focus on.

I'll list out how you can use them as a social media manager and then one example of how you can use them for clients in any niche.

Please note that this isn't something I've come up with on my own but a part of my learnings from an amazing business coach called Cameron Wilke. You can check her out on Instagram @camie.wilke

Now let's dive right into it!

Number1: Pain points. Humans are driven by pain, we are driven by our struggles.

When you highlight the pain points of your ideal client, you show them that you understand them, you know what they need help with.

Examples of content you can create for yourself:

1. How to use hashtags to increase reach?
2. How to create content pillars?

Examples of content you can create for your client:

1. Fitness coach- How to lose weight?
2. Productivity coach- How to manage time?

Number 2: Transformational.

You will see the likes and comments skyrocket when you show before and after

Examples of content you can create for yourself: Feed before working with me vs after optimizing and branding

Examples of content you can create for your client:

Fitness- Personal story of before adopting a healthy lifestyle vs after

Number 3: Storytelling

We all love a good story don't we?

And let's admit it. We all are at least a little nosy.

Examples of content you can create for yourself:

1. Why you decided to be a Social Media Manager
2. What struggles you face along the way

Examples of content you can create for your client:

1. Inspiration drove them to start this business.
2. Their family and friends reaction when they announced it

For product-based-

1. Why the product was made
2. How the design came about
3. What needs it's designed to meet.

Number 4: Educating your audience

Examples of content you can create for yourself:

1. Things you didn't know about hashtags
3. Best timing to post or how to check what time your audience is most active.

Examples of content you can create for your client:

Fitness coach- Difference between carb intake vs protein intake

Mindset coach-3 mindset shifts that will change your life

Number 5: Polarizing i.e. stating your opinions

Examples of content you can create for yourself: Why branding is not the most important aspect to focus on.

Or if you opt for personal, it could be 'Why I don't believe in sexist Indian traditions'

Examples of content you can create for your client:

Fitness coach- Instead of focusing on weight loss, let's learn to take care of our bodies and love them as they are.

Number 6: Common objections you hear

Examples of content you can create for yourself: Is it important to post every single day?

Examples of content you can create for your client: I don't have enough money to invest in your program. List out 5 ways they can make money today and state the importance of getting rid of excuses.

Number 7: Client testimonials and Social Proof

Examples of content you can create for yourself: Insights improvement (you can find this when you click the three lines in the top right corner of your profile. This basically shows the content interactions on the profile)

Examples of content you can create for your client: How they have helped people in the past. Like for a fitness coach it could be test reports of the client or evident weight loss.

Now, what do you do when you have absolutely no social proof? Well, first keep in mind that it's still possible to land clients. Don't let it be a mindset block. When I landed my first client, the only proof I had was my own Instagram page growth and mind you, she was a high paying client.

However, having some social proof is always an advantage so here's how you can go about

1. First, look for people who are in need of your services. You can do this through Facebook groups. But if you're not comfortable with one platform, you can always start off with Instagram or any other that you're

most comfortable with. You're a freelancer. You get to decide your work rules, remember?

2. Once you find your ideal clients, offer some free calls so you build a rapport and then pitch your services either for free or low pay just for the sake of being able to showcase the results. Is it worth it? You may ask. Well, different people have different opinions but I think this is the best way to go.

3. Work really hard to bring in the best possible results. This way there's a high chance they will want to keep you on board for longer even when you raise your prices. But even if not, at least you have some kickass results to show off to other potential clients.

4. Start showing some BTS (Behind the scenes) of what you do. When hiring, clients often want to know how you go about completing the tasks they assign. Showing up consistently and showcasing the tools you use and the systems you have in place can prove more helpful than you think.

Number 8: Bringing Awareness,

Believe it or not, the very first time I did this, I landed my first international client.

YUP! That's the power.

Examples of content you can create for yourself: Introduce yourself and clearly state what your services include as part of a social media manager. Sometimes, people just need to hear something multiple times before they make a decision. Always remember that some people spend spontaneously while there are others who like to take calculated decisions after weighing the pros and cons of both. You need to cater to both and the only way to do so is by consistently showing up to talk about your offer.

Examples of content you can create for your client: Introduce them, their credibility, certifications.

More importantly, effectively communicate their offers in their product suite i.e. a collection of all their different offers like consultation calls, online courses, webinars, etc.

It has to be crisp and clear so that anyone who visits their page will know exactly how and when they can start availing of their offers.

Words to hook your audience through your headline/ first line in your caption:
1. Proven

    Example- 3 proven ways to generate leads for your business.
2. Guaranteed

    Example- Guaranteed way to fast track your success with reels.
3. Full proof

    Example- Your full-proof guide to getting DMs to work for you.
4. Warning

    Example- 3 Warning signs the algorithm is not happy with you.

5. Latest

   Example- Latest Instagram updates you don't want to miss out on.

6. Look

   Example- Look at what I created for you!

7. Special

   Example- July content prompts especially for you.

8. Free

   Example-Free engagement checklist to help you level up with less time.

9. You

   Motivational quotes to help you have a productive day.

10. Easy

    Example- Easy story ideas to save you time

11. Unforgettable.

    Example -Makeup look that will make you unforgettable.

12. Steal

    Example- Steal my engagement strategy.

13. Weird

    Example- Weird but effective ways to increase your growth on Instagram.

14. Confessions

    Example- Confessions of a six-figure business owner.

15. Unbelievable

    Example- An unbelievable way to increase shares of your posts.

16. Ultimate

    Example-Ultimate guide to living a healthy lifestyle.

17. Complete

    Example-A complete library of___

18. Challenge

    Example- 30 day weightloss challenge.

19. Ignore

    Example- 3 Instagram growth myths you need to ignore.

20. Unlock

    Example- Unlock your guide to productivity

Bonus tips:

1. Use numbers- These are great to create expectations. They know exactly how many ways to expect.

2. Ask questions- This helps you get content prompts and also ensures that you're speaking directly to the audience by addressing their pain points. So it's a win-win

3. Focus on the first 3 words+last 3 words. They should make sense by themselves

Headline formulas:

1. How to_____ in _______

    This works well since people are constantly checking for ways to do things on google and if you show them that they can do it in a fixed number of steps, it simplifies things for them.

    Example- How to use hashtags: Everything you need to know to grow through hashtags

Ask yourself what is something your target audience is struggling with or are too afraid to try and create content to simplify things for them

2.   {Do something} like {someone} without {something negative}
Example- Dressing like Priyanka Chopra without breaking your wallet

3.   ____Lessons I learned while___
Example- 10 priceless lessons I learned in years of social media management

4.   _____secrets I learned about____
Example- 3 Secrets I Learnt About Setting Boundaries with clients.

5.   ____ you should know before____
Example- 6 things you should know before starting as a Social Media Manager

As if I haven't given you enough, now here are some done for you, ready to use headlines. I know I'm the best haha.

Educational:

-Steal my hacks to optimize your bio in under 5mins

-CTA hooks that will save hours of your time

-3 Proven Social Media Engagement Strategies

-30 Days content ideas for dentists

-Instagram growth myths you need to ignore

-Complete checklist before you post

-Overrated social media hacks

-3 Things to quit right now when creating reels

-You'll never grow your Instagram until you.

-Highly Engaging story ideas for the week.

-5 Unbelievable ways to get more saves.

-Unlock the 4 Metrics you MUST measure for Social Media Success.

-How to turn followers into paid customers.

-Weird engagement tricks that actually work.

-Steal my content strategy.

-Easy story ideas to save you time.

-What are the key benefits of having an online presence?

-Unlock the 3 best tools to schedule your posts.

-2 Tips to write unforgettable captions.

-Warning: These mistakes are destroying your IG growth.

-3 weird but effective ways to increase your reach.

-5 Tried and tested CTAs that work wonders.

-A story hack you HAVE to be using!

-How to create an aesthetic feed?

Personal
-My monthly goals

-What people think SMMs do vs what we really do

-BTS of you working (Even if it's just for yourself)

-Why I decided to be an SMM

-My simple step- by -step process to create a hashtag bank

-I couldn't grow on Instagram before I knew this

-Struggles I face as an SMM/Confessions of an SMM

-Why you should hire me as an SMM

-A day in the life of a SMM/ a day in my life

-Me when my client asks for the millionth edit

-4 mistakes I made at the beginning of my journey

-My biggest fear as an SMM

-How and why I can be an asset to your business

-Steal my secret to batch creating reels

-My brand new package

-How I learnt buying followers is a TERRIBLE idea

-How I set boundaries as an SMM

When you use up all or most of these, here's a free tool that will come in handy: Title-generator.com

This website is super user friendly. All you have to do is enter one of the words your post includes and there you go! Over 700 catchy headlines are ready for you.

Don't forget to share your post on your story when you use one of these headlines and tag me @carrie.deanna so I can take a look at your amazing work and reshare it with my community!

Now that we've learnt how to begin a post with a bang, let's look at how to end it in a way that helps us, what say?

How do we do this? Through something, we've given the term CTA to.

CTA or Call To Action, like we discussed earlier in the book, is the instruction you give your audience most often at the end of your copy or script.

I'm sure you've heard your favourite YouTube probably say "Don't forget to hit subscribe and smash the bell icon!" right?

Well, that's what a Call To Action is. With so many creators competing for eyeballs, it gets very difficult to get people to do anything. If you don't ask, you don't get it. It's that simple.

At the same time, if you ask for too much, you're likely to get nothing. So never add more than one CTA.

The best way to end your post or caption is to give a very specific step for your audience to take. The success of that post will be determined based on the number of people who have paid attention to that step.

For example- "Like if you found value in this post. "
If you add this CTA, you will judge the performance of your post based on the number of likes regardless of whether or not people have commented, saved or shared.

But if you say "Share with a friend who needs to hear this!", you will look for the number of shares and judge accordingly. This is how you know whether your audience takes you seriously or you've been friend-zoned.

Another thing to keep in mind is to give a very specific action wherever possible.
Ex: "Comment below with 'Yes' if you agree." instead of just "Comment below."
When you simplify the process as much as possible for the person, they are way more likely to follow through.

Bonus tip: Remember the law of reciprocity. People are open to giving when they receive since they are thankful. So you've got to try and remind them.
Example- "Comment below with ' ' if this quote motivated you."

We have included the part that says 'if this motivated you' just to remind them what you have already done for them making it way more likely for them to be grateful and do something for you in return.

There are mainly two types of call to action.

The ones we've discussed above are what we call engagement CTAs. These are used most often.

Some common examples-

1. Did you find this relatable? Comment below.
2. Do you struggle with staying consistent too?
3. Don't forget to save this as a reminder for later!
4. Double tap if you agree.

The other kind called sales CTAs is used for promotional posts.

Let's look at a couple of examples-

1. Click the link in my bio to sign up!
2. If you find yourself overwhelmed with the process of content creation, perhaps you need a social media manager. Drop 'Overwhelmed' in the comments below and I'll get in touch with you!
3. The first 3 people to book a consultation call with me get a flat 30% off. DM to grab your spot NOW.

Although coaches often use this during launches and you can too when you launch your 1:1 consultation calls or a course but make sure to use them every once in a while on promotional posts too. I got 2 international leads simply due to my solid CTAs on promotional posts.

Why you shouldn't edit your Instagram posts:
Did you know that when you edit your post, all likes and comments up until that point are then disregarded by the algorithm?

This means you will be taken out of the top posts list.

So what can you do instead?

Nothing! We're human and we all make mistakes, let it go. If it's bothering you weeks from then, when the engagement stops on that particular post, then go ahead and make the changes.

That being said, if it hasn't been very long and you notice an error almost immediately after posting it, you can make the edit since it's not so much of a problem if Instagram doesn't consider the few likes so far.

Post sizes
Have you ever noticed some people posting rectangular posts?

Wondered if they don't know the Instagram requirements?

Well, it's quite the contrary. Instagram feed posts should be 1080×1350 px NOT the typical 1080×1080.

Why? Well, this is simply because you want to take up as much space on someone's screen as possible.
The algorithm will then know the person has a high level

of interest in your content thus pushing your future posts too and pushing the same ones to more people.

Now, all that said, beware of the fact that if you place a picture of someone's face at the ends, it's likely to get cut off in the feed when someone visits your profile.

So when designing, make sure all your info and important graphics are within 1080×1080 but the overall sizing is 1080×1350.

The same goes for reels. Far too many people make the mistake of adding text too high or too low which often then gets cut off in the feed and looks very unprofessional.

Pro tip: when posting reels, there's an option to crop profile photos, click on that and adjust the cover so you know what exactly will be visible when it appears in your feed layout.

Always always always post your reels to your feed. More eyeballs the better right?

One common question that I'd like to address: How do I decide what to post and what to save for paid programs?

If you've started your content creation journey and have some kind of digital product as well like a course or an ebook, very often there's a conflict between the amount of value to provide for free vs the amount to save for your paid program.

I get it, I've been there myself. But one call that turned things around for me was with a business coach who told me the basic rule.

You post 'What' your audience needs to do to solve a particular problem they're facing.
In your paid program, you teach the 'How'. It's just that simple.
For example- you post on your feed the importance of optimizing one's profile but in your course or ebook, you take them through the process of actually doing everything involved step by step.

That's all that it is. Doesn't have to be complicated!

Story strategy
My absolute favourite part of Instagram is stories. Here's why:

1. Stories don't have any rules or limitations. You can literally post ANYYYTHINGG from a picture of your cat to 2417339237 reasons why you don't believe in something. People will hear you out no matter what the topic. But on your feed, it's limited to your niche.
2. There are so many interesting features like GIFs, music, question stickers and polls to increase engagement.
3. You can use it to conduct market research or even ask anything that you're struggling with. Once I remember I was having trouble making the payment for Canva pro and asked if anyone knew what to do,

guess what? Not only did I get a ton of people giving me solutions but I had one follower who gave me access to her Canva pro group for FREE! How cool is that?

4. You can show up in your night suit and nobody will say a thing. It doesn't require you to be all decked up and formal.

5. You can post anytime in the day. It doesn't have to be when your audience is most active cause if you post every 2-3hrs, it will keep showing up anyway to your audience thus increasing visibility.

6. Mini training can help acquire the best of clients even later when saved to highlights. I've lost count of the number of people who have texted me showing appreciation for the value I share in my stories and highlights. So many clients who weren't sure at one point converted after viewing my stories since it gave them the reassurance they needed.

The list is endless, to be honest but I think you get my point. You cannot, just CANNOT afford to miss out on stories when they have the power to do so much.

Here are some things to keep in mind that will help you post better stories:

1. Always address just one person so they feel like you're talking specifically to them. Example- Hey you! Hope you're having a wonderful day. Wanted to help you with anything you've been struggling with so here's a question sticker to put in any questions you have that I'd love to answer here in my stories." A lot

of people make the mistake of making their script very impersonal by starting with "Hey everyone!"

2. When you reshare someone else's post or even your own for that matter, specify why they should check it out. This is important, especially for video content. For carousels, if your headline is catchy enough, it won't require much else to get them to tap.

3. Share bits of your life. People are very nosy. They love to know what's going on with you so don't shy away from talking about your experiences, learnings, daily struggles or even just your hobbies. All of this helps build a personal brand.

4. Add subtitles to your stories, preferably static although you can add live captions by shooting your stories on reels, adding the live captions using the feature there and then downloading it to your device and uploading to stories. If you really don't have the time to type then this is better than nothing but static captions perform the best since they are easier to read and less time-consuming.

5. Compress the text as much as possible. Have smaller sizes as well as fewer words or else it looks like a kids story book.

6. Add question stickers and polls in the middle of the screen as far as possible and make sure they aren't too small. A lot of people make a mistake of adding them

in the corners which makes it difficult to tap. Most common mistake is people putting it so low that when you try tapping on it, you get an option to send the person a message instead.

7. Have a good balance of 60-40% where 60% is niche relevant and 40% is personal. This is mainly when trying to build a personal brand so it wouldn't apply for product-based clients but definitely applicable for yourself.

8. Use your brand colors when adding text to your stories. This helps people associate your brand colors to you. You can either move the paintbrush approximately in the area of the color or add an image (one of your posts that has your brand colors on it) to your story and place the paintbrush on the part that has the color you want to add.

9. Try and promote other people's posts on your stories and make sure to tag them. While this is a good way to encourage people and share value, it can also help you get visibility if the person reshares it to their feed. It also makes it more likely for the person to reshare one of your posts.

10. Pro tip: Show up ALL THE TIME during launch periods. Your stories should be full of questions being answered, reasons why they should sign up, testimonials of people who have signed up, etc. An average Instagram user may have to see something

upto 12 times before they actively recognize what they're seeing. It can then take additional 7-19 times before they are open to invest. Crazy? I know, but I didn't make this up myself.

Now that we know all the tips and tricks let's look at the exact content that you can start posting to get started with. I've listed out a few prompts that will help you kickstart your journey whether it's from scratch or starting back after a break, I'm sure these will come in handy.

No more worrying or wondering what to post.

Here's a done for you 30 day plan that you can use every month:

Day 1: Picture of your workspace.

Day 2: Favorite creator and biggest lesson learnt from them.

Day 3: Picture of you when small and what advice you'd like to give your younger self.

Day 4: 3 things you're most grateful for today + Question sticker asking your audience the same.

Day 4: A picture of a family vacation + Importance of taking breaks (google it haha).

Day 5: favourite festival and why.

Day 6: A joke.

Day 7: Throwback to your last birthday and shoutout to a friend/ family member who made it extra special.

Day 8: Celebrate your wins.

Day 9: Most important person in your life + why.

Day 10: A pet you currently own/ owned and the advantage of having pets/that particular pet.

Day 11: Favourite sport and why.

Day 12: Important reminder.

Day 13: Best quote you've read.

Day 14: How many languages do you know? Which all? How did you learn them? Ask your audience how many they know as well.

Day 15: 3 favourite books and one thing you took back from anyone.

Day 16: If I could live without rules for one day, I would _______________ Then ask what they would do as well and share the interesting answers.

Day 17: Quiz on yourself (Include some things you posted about in the previous days to see whos actively watching your stories)

Day 18: favourites colour and what it symbolizes.

Day 19: My worst habit.

Day 20: A song that helps you calm down.

Day 21: The biggest mistake you've made so far.

Day 22: favourite podcast and one thing you learnt from it .

Day 23: Biggest lesson my mom/ dad taught me.

Day 24: favourite YouTuber.

Day 25: If you had a six-figure business, what would you use the money for?

Day 26: A funny incident you had in college.

Day 27: An investment that paid off + importance of investing in learning.

Day 28: favourites Hindi song.

Day 29: One regret.

Day 30: One thing I miss most about school. Ask them what they miss.

You can get images from Pinterest or Pixabay and as I mentioned earlier, don't forget to include a lot of polls and engaging stickers asking them for their opinion.

Note that most of the prompts are on the personal side so make sure to include mini trainings and educational stories at least twice a week too.

Prompts that you can use for market research through stories:

1. What's one thing you're struggling with the most right now?

2. What qualities do you look for in a coach/ service provider/ product?
3. Would you prefer a lower price but lower returns or a higher price with guaranteed amazing returns?
4. If you could make a wish today to improve something about your business, what would it be?

Bonus tip: Create weekly themes around each day. This has helped make things so much easier, especially when creating stories for clients.

Here's an example:

Mini training Monday- Start the week with some value for your audience.

Transformational Tuesday- Share your client layout transformation before and after working with you or any client wins.

Working Wednesday- Show some behind the scenes of your work.

Thoughtful Thursday- Ask your audience for their opinion on something by putting up a question sticker and then sharing their responses.

Freak out Friday- Take a break from stories and focus on finishing off work before the weekend.

Siesta Saturday- Talk about your weekend plans and perhaps have a quiz about you so your audience can get to know you better.

Shameless Sunday-Keep one day flexible. Maybe you can share some self-care practices that you do on weekends or if you're feeling productive, share something valuable you learnt during the week.

Hope these themes help you organize things and come up with more creative ideas for yourself and your clients as well.

But of course, we know that to grow on Instagram, simply creating content isn't gonna do the trick. The key to building a good follower base and network is to be able to engage with your audience well regularly.

So here are some steps to getting your engagement game strong.

BOULDER-

1. The first 30mins after you post are crucial and decide how far Instagram will push your post so make sure to share your post on your stories directing people to engage. Log in from all other accounts that you handle as well and like and comment on those.

2. Reply to comments on your post within the first one hour. The rest can be left for the next time you post. This helps them keep thinking of you and hence makes it way more likely for them to check out your feed to see if you have anything new.

3. Reply to comments with questions. This will prompt them to answer thus increasing the number of

comments. Example: If your post is about '3 ways to increase your reach on Instagram', and they comment saying "Amazing post", reply saying "So glad you agree! Which point did you like best?"

4. Respond to people's question stickers and they will make sure to respond to yours.

5. Follow and DM at least 5 ideal clients on a daily basis and try to make conversations with them. DO NOT pitch until you have established a strong relationship first.

6. Go to the 5 hashtags you use regularly and comment on the first 8 posts that appear.
    Not just with emojis, drop genuine comments that give you a chance to get pinned.
    If you don't know what pinning of comments is, it's basically when a creator wants your comment to stay first even if 100 people commented before and after you.

7. Pin comments on your own posts and put up stories that make them known to your audience. This will make it more likely for them to comment on your posts knowing there's a chance of getting a reward of being pinned that will give them exposure to your audience.

8. Use voice notes in DMs. Don't worry about sounding perfect, don't worry at all about being professional.

Have natural conversations just like you're talking to your best friend. Hearing your voice will help them feel more connected to you.

9. Go back to old posts and check the ones who used to comment frequently but don't anymore. It's time to revive some old friendships. Slide into their DMs and find out how they're doing.

And that's about it. I know it seems like a lot but highlight one or two points per day and practice a few at a time. Slowly but surely, it'll become a habit.

These strategies will help you grow your following. Now, I know a lot of experts go about saying "Followers don't matter." And before you hate me, hear me out.

I agree it's true. But only on some level.
If you want to get your first client, followers don't matter.
If you want to hit 50k as a freelancer, followers don't matter.
If you want to launch your 1:1 calls, followers don't matter.

So when do they matter then?
If you want to pitch to big brands, followers can help build a better impression.
If you want to have clients on the waitlist, followers give them the assurance that your services are worth waiting for.
If you want to start with paid promotions, followers do

matter when you go to pitch.

Think about a restaurant that's packed. Why do people still stand out waiting in a line even when they can easily go to another one considering there are so many that are half-empty? The number of people is in a way an indication that the food is good.

We can't run away from the fact that quantity does matter. All we need to remind ourselves is that quality quantity is what's required.

Yes, 10 genuine followers are better than 100 bots. But 100 genuine followers are better than 10 right? There's no denying that.

Now on, let's be open about the fact that we're trying to grow. One metric to measure growth is followers. This doesn't mean I'm against removing bot accounts just for the sake of numbers. I do a regular cleanse myself to ensure all my followers are real.

But what I'm trying to stress on is to take engagement seriously. That's one practice that will help you grow and reach out to some really great people across the globe who,fingers crossed, will follow you and cheer you on in your journey.

DM strategy
I am a huge believer that DMs are where sales are born.

Yes content is great, yes showing up consistently can take you a long way. But now more than ever with all content creators competing for eyeballs, it's more and more difficult to sell through content.

Our attention spans have decreased, there's no denying that.

So the best way to get 1:1 attention and have genuine conversations in the DMs.

Only when I started getting active in my DMs was I able to make sales. Be it 1:1 consultations or Social Media Clients. Want to know exactly how?

Steal my secret C-C-W-U-F formula-

1. Compliment

As much as you love talking about yourself, you've got to remember that people only care about themselves.

So start not with flattery but with a genuine compliment about their feed.

It could be a specific post you found value in or it could be you commending their consistency.

Here's an example- Hey Tyler! Just came across your profile and I have to say I absolutely love your work. You have such a beautiful feed. Really looking forward to learning more from you and growing together. Don't hesitate to let me know if you need any kind of help. Have a great day!

I have only got positive responses from this so far. People are so touched that you took out the time from your busy schedule only to send in such a sweet text.

2. Commonality

Then start a conversation asking them simple questions about their business and find something in common. This will help build trust.

Example- I see that you started your journey about 3 months back just like me. That's so cool! How has your journey been so far?

3. Warm up

Introduce yourself and talk about your services. Since you've already asked them about their business first, it won't seem salesy.

Example- I love that you coach people who have mindset issues. It really is the need of the hour. I decided to take up Social Media Management for similar reasons. I do feel like a lot of businesses benefit a great deal when they have a strong social media presence, don't you agree?

4. Urgency

Be more specific with the transformation you can bring to their business. Include emotion whenever possible.

Example- It gives me so much joy when my clients make sales after applying the strategies I suggest.

5. Free call

Invite them to a coffee chat with you where you can help them with something they're struggling with and then pitch formally.

Example- I'd love to get on a call with you to catch up. I noticed that you don't use a lot of hashtags in your posts. That could be hurting your growth so perhaps I could help you with that as well during the call?

That's basically it! My simple secret sauce.

If you're chatting with multiple potential clients, I'd highly recommend using a simple lead tracker.

Just create a google sheet with the person's name, date of 1ˢᵗ DM, date of compliment, etc. (each of the 5 stages)

BOULDER: Perform all the tasks above using my signature framework.

Few pointers to keep in mind:

1. Remember to go into DMs relaxed. Don't put too much pressure on yourself to be too formal. Treat it just like any other conversation you'd have with a friend.

2. Whenever possible, send voice notes. The kind of connection you can build

when someone hears you out (literally) is incomparable to the friendship built over simple texts.

3. Reply to their stories once in a while and comment on their posts as well.

4. Whenever you use a question sticker in your own stories, use it as an opportunity to start a conversation with everyone who engages with it.

   Although I highly recommend genuine conversations, it can get boring to keep typing the same thing that repeats in most conversations like how you started your freelancing journey, how it's going so far, where you're from, what you do, etc.
   So in order to speed things up and avoid getting bored of small talk, it's best to have saved replies at hand.

   In case you haven't heard of this before, saved replies are an option on the right when texting. You can just tap on it and add a chunk of text with a shortcut word that will serve as a prompt whenever you need to use it.

Hashtag strategy
Success is a stepping stone to success and NO that isn't a typo.

Now before you pounce on me, hear me out.

Agreed, failure is a stepping stone to success too but in the field of social media, with things like hashtags, what performs well is what allows you to model on.

Think about it, we can very well look at which hashtags haven't performed well on our previous posts. But from there, can we determine what will do well?

Now moving to a post that has got great reach all thanks to hashtags. This particular post will show you exactly what works. You can not only use the same set of hashtags off and on but check the ratio of sizes, types, etc.

All things said, I have to admit that in the beginning, I really didn't get it. Not in the first week nor the first month.

How are hashtags put together? Why are there a million tools and how do I know which one is the best?

Don't you worry, if there's any sort of confusion with hashtags right now, I'm sure by the end of this chapter, you'll have utmost clarity.

To begin with, the simplest rule to keep in mind is not to use any hashtags over 1M and less than 10k. These will either be over-saturated or nobody's even looking at them.

How many? Well Instagram keeps changing its rule. Even though 30 is the limit, Instagram recommends 7-15 as of now and it could change in a couple of years or even months.

But here are some things that will stay the same:
1. Use location based hashtags- I'm putting this first since a huge majority of people don't use any.
2. Have at least one or two personal hashtags. Something that is unique to your brand be it your own name or brand name.
3. Use at least 5 specific hashtags. These are in detail hashtags to do with the particular post. Based on the content shared, look for hashtags that are bigger than 10k and smaller than 3M.
4. Have a variety of different sizes and keep experimenting to see which do best on each account. Every client's account will be different. The same hashtags won't work for all. More often than not it's a hit and miss. But don't be discouraged.

Remember to keep your hashtag banks handy so you can keep adding them each time you post and alternate between each of them. Either have them in your notes or in a Google sheet.

In my opinion, while hashtags can give a fairly good reach, I don't believe they deserve too much time from our end. There's no guarantee. The only three things that will guarantee success on Social media are value, engagement and consistency.

Comment strategy

I know you've never heard this before so get ready for a strategy that's going to help you be visible to thousands of borrowed audiences.

BOULDER-

Here's how you can get your comments pinned on big accounts of content creators in your industry:

1. Look for 3-5 accounts that have a huge part of their following consisting of your ideal clients.

2. Turn on their post notifications so you're one of the first to comment thus increasing the chances of appearing on the top.

3. Think carefully about what the message is you're trying to put across. Take into consideration what your ideal clients will resonate with and what will hopefully spark a conversation.

4. Stalk the account to identify the loyal followers who comment regularly and start liking their comments. In turn, they will like yours thus showing the account owner that your comment is pin-worthy.

I know it seems like quite a bit of work but think about how many people could potentially see your comment and flood your DMs with enquiries that could generate thousands of dollars in revenue.

Checking Insights

For many of us, insights may seem scary to even dive into, but we've all started from scratch now, haven't we? In this chapter, I will talk briefly about most of the things that you need to know in order to be able to track your insights and then make progress using them.

The first step, of course, is to find your insights.

How do you do this?

1. When you go to your Instagram profile and find three lines on the top right and click on them, you get the option of Insights.
2. Tap on the inside button that will take you to a screen that will show you a basic overview. The first metric available is accounts reached. Here, you will get an idea as to how many people you have been reaching out to through your posts in the last 30 days.
3. Then comes the accounts engaged. This is what determines how many people have actively commented, liked or shared your post. It could also be referring to the number of people who have replied to your stories and DMs.
4. The total number of followers is basically an increase in the following account in the past month.
5. You then move on to see the content that you have shared, the stories that you have shared and insights of particular posts like reels videos, annual lights, that's all, isn't it?

Insights never have to be complicated, and tracking them can do. We can take your business to a whole new level.

But yet, I could never!

Neither did I know what updates the client would be interested in, nor did I know how exactly to track insights at the beginning of my journey.

If only someone had told me straight, I'd have managed to retain so many more clients that I lost since I couldn't meet their expectations.

So, here are a few things you can keep in mind that will for sure help you ensure a better client experience:

1. The first few weeks are THE MOST IMPORTANT part of the journey. The trust you earn in this period is what will help them stick along even if things get messy somewhere down the line. So, it's best to give a lot of attention to a client in the beginning stages. This is why I always have at least 15 days of a gap between taking on new clients, and I'd highly recommend the same for you.

I remember early on in my journey, my first ever client had the best experience for the first month. She loved my work ethic, content, designs, everything. But when I started getting more clients and trying to juggle everything, I wasn't able to keep myself to the standard.

She still had the patience and stuck with me though cause

she knew from the first month that I had the potential.

2. Send in a text at least every alternate day, if not daily giving them-updates as to what's happening or sometimes maybe it's just to ask for approval. The goal is to have a conversation going so they know you're putting in the work. Often, what happens is no matter how much effort you're putting in behind the scenes, if you don't communicate, it somehow seems to the client like you aren't giving their account the attention they desire.

What I do is in order to give them that reassurance, I get on a call with them every once in a while to see if there's any particular area they need changes in or any way I can improve. I'm always open to constructive criticism.

Sometimes, we get so used to the way we do things that we are blinded by the ways we falter. So, having someone call you out helps improve for the better. While your business friends can do it too, it's always more honest when it comes from a client since they're shelling out money.

3. Have a sheet to track the analytics.
To be honest, I hate this part. Not even going to try and hide it.
I can barely to this date stay consistent in terms of tracking so what I do is I sit down on one particular day and get it all done together.

Depending on what suits you best, you can decide how

you want to go about it. Either you can spend 4-5mins daily or about 70-90mins once a month.

What you've got to track is basically the insights of each post. I use Google sheets but you're free to use Excel. I'd recommend one of the two. Most clients are familiar with these common ones. When you use any other, even though they're more convenient at times, there really is no point when in the end the client is unable to understand, and doesn't have the time or patience to figure it out.

Now moving to what the actual task is.
What you've got to do is basically go to the insights of each post and write down the number of likes, comments, shares, saves, follows, impressions and anything else you may find useful. This will not only help the client see the results your work is bringing to the account but help you figure out what kind of posts bring what kind of traction. You can then focus on creating more similar content.

4. Check, if they prefer your long captions or short and many different slides in their carousels or just 2-3.
There are some clients that prefer short captions in general. They want the focus to be mainly on the graphic or video. In that case, spending those extra minutes or hours on writing captions is just a waste of time.
Similarly, there are some who prefer shorter pieces of content while others want it a little longer.

Ultimately, you've got to give them what they want. Many people tend to project their own content consuming patterns onto everyone else. I had a client who never read long captions so she thought no one else does either and she asked me to skip it. Another client never slides through carousels so she asked me to avoid more than 3 slides.

Of course there are some great clients who trust your judgment and allow for flexibility but there are others who want things done their way and even if you don't think it will give them the best results, communicating doesn't help much cause they've made up their mind.

I've had my fair share of these kinds of clients. The funny thing is one was into counselling. Really weird how she was able to guide other people when she herself had such a terrible way of dealing.

Anyway, what I realized (a little too late) is that it's best to find a sweet spot that both parties agree on and that will bring decent results at the least.

Instagram cleanse:
-Remove all bot followers.
These are basically the accounts with no profile picture whose ratio of followers to following is disproportionate in the sense that they follow way more people than those who follow them.

-Delete all comments from random people who are come to pass their time and have no real interest in your content. The algorithm will push your content to more such people, if you encourage engagement from them.

We're all guilty of leaving messages unseen. For some of us, it's 1, for others it's 100. But before stepping into the new year, make sure you respond to all old texts so you aren't anxious with the numbers pilling up. And who knows? Maybe your next client is waiting in there for you.

-Delete all unnecessary saved posts. Let's face it. How often do we keep saving things we think we'll go back to but never really make use of? Deleting the old will help you make space for the new that you'll probably make use of and even if you don't, less clutter can never possibly be a bad thing right?

-Segregate the necessary posts into folders. Yes! This feature is available on Instagram. Go to the three lines on the right of your home page, click on save and you'll see an additional symbol on the top right. Click on there and add any posts you want to be put together.
Instagram does move things around from time to time, so when you read this year after I've written on it, please don't come at me.

Phone cleanse:
If you've been into social media management for even a few weeks now, you definitely know why a cleanse every once in a while is so important.
I'm a minimalist in general but I'm definitely not going to ask you to clean your room and get rid of things you haven't used in months. I am however going to encourage

you to arrange your folders, chats, gallery (ESPECIALLY GALLERY!) on both your phone and laptop but mainly phone.

BOULDER:
1. Delete all unnecessary photos that you just took to send someone in the moment.
Simple!
2. Go to your screenshots and select all images that you need as references for your clients.
3. Create a new folder with all these and then one by one segregate them further into one folder for each client.
4. Go to the camera and select everything that could possibly be used in your Instagram stories. Again, create a separate folder called 'stories'.
5. Check your list of downloads. Get rid of all the unnecessary files that show up.
6. Go to your audio recordings and filter them out.

That's about it! While there are things you could add, it's best to start with just 3-4 of these steps. Once you build the momentum, you'll start getting more organized.

HOW TO PREVENT BURNOUT

"Are you kidding? Why would I ever get bored of something I'm so passionate about?"

These were my exact words the first time I watched an Instagram live on dealing with burnout.

In the beginning, any new venture seems fun. I will never forget my first few weeks. There were days I'd honestly be able to sit down for 5-6hrs at a stretch to brainstorm and come up with fancy content ideas.

But a couple of weeks down the line, I faced major burnout which got me to the point where I started to question if this is even the right field for me.

If this hasn't happened to you yet, I can assure you that it's very likely to get exhausted with creating content not just for yourself but for your clients as well if you overdo things in the beginning. Thankfully, there are several great ways to systematically create content that won't need hours of your time daily.

First, you need to reflect on the kind of person that you are, and know your limits.

Are you someone with a lack of focus who can only work a few minutes at a time?

If so, you need to set 1hr in the morning, 1hr in the afternoon and 1hr, late evening for 3-5days and you can batch create content for the month.

If you're someone who really enjoys the process and can sit with it for hours at the end (which is what I personally prefer cause when I get in the zone, creativity just flows), then set aside the last day of every month to plan for the next month.

How exactly you can go about with the content creation process is discussed in detail in the following chapter.

Another way to prevent burnout is to have a limit for each task, and switch to something else once you've crossed it. A limit can be set either in terms of hours spent or the number. Example: My limit of screen time is 3hrs. When I hit 3hrs, I need to either go out for a walk or spend time with family. Sometimes I just keep to myself and clear my room but no screen time for at least 20mins.

Further, within those 3hrs I set a number on each thing like a number of reels I can watch at a stretch is 15. After that, I need to switch tasks.

These are numbers I've found to work best for me over time. Don't just blindly copy the same. Figure out what works for you by making some adjustments and trying out new ways.

Okay, now the next one is going to seem like a no-brainer but far too many people (like me) don't take this seriously enough and so, I have to mention it…TAKE AT LEAST ONE DAY OFF per week and communicate that effectively with friends and family. Thank me later!

But now for some real talk, no matter what you try doing, sometimes burnout is inevitable. We all have a fixed period. If we go anything beyond, it backfires. I've realized that it's 4 months for me. So every 4 months, I need time off, be it a vacation or just letting go of some clients to make time for other things that excite me.

BOULDER:

1. Note down things that light your soul on fire. It may be singing, painting, travelling, helping those in need, anything at all that leaves you with a feeling of deep satisfaction.
2. Track how often you face burnout. If it's every 3 months, make sure in every 2.5 months, you take at least a week off to make time for these activities.

Trust me, when you schedule breaks from time to time, you prevent forced breaks at unwanted times due to burnout. I've been there way too often. I hope this exercise will make sure you don't go there as often or in fact not at all.

Another effective hack is to separate work and rest environments. Work from your desk, rest on your bed.

I'm definitely not a good example of this cause I love working from my bed but I've been making an effort of late to try and limit that. Our brains get the signal to shut off when in a particular environment. If we start mixing things up, we stop feeling sleepy on the bed and start getting in work mode instead which messes up our whole sleep cycle then.

Finally, being a math student, I love formulas so this is something I've devised over time that helps me prevent burnout:

Fulfilment-Strain= Energy

In order to preserve your energy, you need to either increase the time spent in things that bring you a sense of fulfilment or decrease the things that are causing a strain in your life. The choice is yours. It's ultimately up to you to strike the right balance.

Another thing I thought would be important to mention cause how I wish someone told me this earlier is when you work, work. When you play, play. Don't mix the two.

When you work, be all in.
When you're spending time with family, be fully present. Don't mix the two. Never take your laptop to the dining table. Never check client work when out at the playground.

For the longest time I let my work life affect my relationship with my family. I'd get annoyed with them when they wanted to go out often, I'd resent them for not taking their life 'as seriously' as me cause they weren't running a business and wouldn't understand what I'm going through.

But I soon realized that those were just excuses. I was just hiding behind work. There was something bothering me and instead of dealing with it, I'd just keep myself busy all the time which is why idle time annoyed me.

When I worked on inner healing and finally was at peace with myself, everything fell into place. I was able to lend a helping hand to my mum when she needed it, spent quality time with my dad and sister and tried to play with my little brother often.

Life goes by so quickly but if you set aside time for the things that truly matter, you start seeing the beauty of the little things.

SLAYING ON FACEBOOK

I'm no expert.

I really know nothing about the Facebook algorithm. When you figure it out, please let me know.

But in this chapter, what I will be focusing on is what I do know.

Instagram is a more visual platform but Facebook and LinkedIn are places where you could just be a decent writer and that's all you would need to be consistent with posting.

So, here's a simple formula to keep in mind:

I call it my very own S-E-A formula.

S-Surprise: In less than 7 words, hook them onto your post with something unusual or controversial.

E-Educate/ Entertain: You then go on to either educate them or entertain them with a funny, relatable story to build a connection.

A-Action: Every piece of content must have a goal-based on which you give a strong Call To Action for your audience to do something in return.

Let's look at an example:

Don't show up consistently on stories! (Surprise)

Who needs sales? Why do we need clients?

Our business is functional without them too right?

Haha, caught you by surprise, didn't I?

We both know consistency is key to success on social media.

So quit sitting on the couch and go shoot that mini-training you've been thinking of for the past week.

Comment below with "On it" if this inspired you. (Action)

There you go. A short and sweet caption that starts with a statement contrary to what we know, then moves on to help them relate and ends with inspiring them to take action.

Don't forget to sprinkle some emojis to just spice up your content a little bit.

Let's move on to see what other kinds of posts you can put out on Facebook-

Facebook content types:

1. Images

2. Video
3. Blogs
4. Links
5. Shared posts
6. Dark posts
7. FB Live

A few tips to help you curate content:

1. Follow industry leaders for inspiration. DON'T COPY, just model on their content.

2. Find a few topics that your ideal audience is interested in. This may have nothing to do with your product or services in particular.

3. Ask questions to your audience, this always increases engagement. On days that you lack creativity or you're just busy, put out a simple post with a question asking for people's opinion.

4. Have a unique and consistent brand voice and tone. If you're the bold, assertive type, stick to that so people respect you. If you have a playful tone, make sure you're consistent in every copy and people will slowly start being able to find you fun and relatable. There's nothing wrong with any tone, you just need to be able to stay consistent with it.

5. Don't post links, instead put them in the first comment and create an image about what the link is. Facebook decreases the reach of links since it senses

that you're trying to send your audience out of their platform

Tools to curate content:

1.   Google industry alerts
2.   Google trends
3.   Scoop It
4.   Buzz Sumo
5.   Facebook audience insights
6.   Facebook trends
7.   Facebook debugger

Tools you need to improve efficiency

If I'm being honest, tools scare the living hell out of me. I fear learning to use new software. But, if you're anything like me, please push yourself to learn cause it can cost you, clients.

Let me tell you how I lost a client who had a following of 17,000 just because I didn't know how to edit videos decently.

I was super excited to work with a big account but I had no idea the amount of effort it would involve to edit reels neither did I know it was possible on canva. I had only used a little of the app caller 'Inshot' up to that point.

There were 2 reels due on one particular day and I hunted for reel editors all over. On Facebook groups, Instagram, asking friends if they knew anyone, so on and so forth.

In the end, I had to pay them 3 times what I was being paid which was a huge loss for me and guess what? The client didn't like any of them. She ended up editing the reel herself.

After that day, I let go of the client and focused on first getting better at basic tools like in shot, canva, notion, Trello, etc.

So here's your next **BOULDER:**

-Play around with Inshot for resizing and editing reels. You can get a ton of free tutorials on YouTube.

-Experiment with Trello in order to share boards so that the client has a proper understanding of what the status is and doesn't have to keep asking. Trust me, this tool is way easier than you can imagine.

-DO NOT NEGLECT THIS: Try Creator Studio for scheduling. I took this tool for granted for a very long time until I hired my amazing Virtual Assistant to help me out with the same and it has taken a huge load off my chest.

Designing tips and tricks

Not my cup of tea at all!

I honestly never thought I could design those kinds of elite looking Instagram layouts or Facebook posts that big creators put out.
I settled on being just good enough. Nothing out of the blue, nothing extraordinary until… I put my foot down.

If I wanted to be able to work with high paying clients, I would need to offer services that deserved to be paid high.

So I got down to learning canva in depth.
I sat for hours experimenting with various elements, learnt how to add shadows, layering, animation,etc.

While there were some decent YouTube tutorials, I couldn't really find any that would show the kind of layouts I was aiming towards designing.

So, all I did was go to Pinterest and take some inspiration. I created a board of Instagram templates inspiration and tried to imitate things here and there until I found my style not too long ago.

Here are some designing tips I was given along the way by my designer friends so pay careful attention:

1. Avoid right alignment when you're typing in English or any language that's read from left to right. You either left align or let it be centre aligned. This makes it way easier to read.

2. Look for elements like a shadow and add them in some places to give a 3D effect.

3. Use the logo or tag the brand in the centre or extreme right when designing and make sure it's positioned the same in every post.

4. Decide on certain elements and stick to them for a particular brand. Having a set of brand elements in place makes things easier and the feed looks cohesive as well.

5. Make sure not to add too many elements in one post and try to put your posts together to check the layout(this is specifically for Instagram) before you post. If it hits the eye, modify the posts accordingly.

6. Have fonts designated to each kind of texts. For your headings, pick a particular font and always stick to it. For the body, there will be a different one but ensure that it complements the heading. An easy way to pick is to just type free canva font combinations on Pinterest and you'll have a whole list to choose from.

7. Skip a weight when it comes to font. Go from light to bold or from medium to extra bold when changing font weights. The key to great design is contrast. Slight changes in weight change make it harder for the audience to notice the difference.

8. Don't leave the widow. Avoid having a single word on the last line of a paragraph. This is generally referred to as the widow.

9. Spacing matters. The closer things are together, the more the reader will assume a relationship exists between separate blocks of information.

10. Use contrasting colours. As obvious as it sounds, I see a tonne of people making the mistake of using very

similar shades in designs. One light and one dark is way less likely to go wrong compared to both dark or both light.

11..Make sure there isn't too much text in one slide. Let your text breathe, don't use too many elements around either. Often, it's less that's more classy.

12. Avoid corners. Negative space is actually a good thing. It allows your design to breathe a little so don't place elements along the edge or corners of a page.

Please note, I've learnt some of these points from the YouTube channel called 'The Futur'. Take a look at their channel and more others to learn about designing in-depth. These points are a few basics to keep in mind.

I wouldn't advise canva pro for the first few months but when you do have a steady stream of clients coming in and you need to level up, definitely consider opting for the paid subscription so you can save the brand kits of your clients and your own as well thus making the designing process so much shorter and less time consuming.

Now that we've got the tech side of things out of the way, let's look at how you can start reaching out to people after your content game is strong.

How to network:
Almost every opportunity that I've got today is a result of networking.
From my first high paying client and the first international client to my designer for this book, I found the best people

to help me in my journey only because I openly spoke to as many people as I possibly could in the online space.

I know it seems scary at first. Trust me, it was completely out of my comfort zone. In school, I barely had any friends believe it or not. I had no friendship bands at the end of friendship day. I still remember picking up a band from the floor and putting it on in 3rd grade just so my parents would think I have at least one friend.
So, take it from one of the least social people, it's possible to get comfortable out of your comfort zone.

Just challenge yourself to talk to at least 5 new people daily and in a matter of a few weeks, you'll turn into a social pro.

Not saying it doesn't give me anxiety at all anymore. Till date, going to weddings and meeting a bunch of new people gives me anxiety but I push through the first few difficult minutes. I start making a conversation and look for things that interest the other person.

Always make sure to talk about things that the other person is passionate about. In fact, some of the best conversations are when you're only asking questions. When you see their eyes light up, dig deeper, ask for more details, more stories and they'll be happy to tell you more about the subject. Trust me, by the end of the conversation they'll end up feeling like you're some long lost friend.

I learned some more really great tips from 'How to Win

Friends and Influence People' by Dale Carnegie. I highly recommend the book. Check it out right after you're done with this. From using people's names as often as possible to avoiding conflict cause you can never really win a conversation, this book is packed with value.

I'll leave you with the famous quote that I'm sure you've probably come across at some time. But I just want you to know that I believe in it 100% and that is 'Your network is your net worth'.

On the next page, let's look at how you can price your services.

HOW MUCH TO CHARGE

"Just give me anything you can spare!". I know nobody uses these exact words but most newbie social media managers or just freelancers in general enter the industry with this attitude.

When starting off, it doesn't seem like we have much of a choice as to how much to charge right? Anything, literally ANYTHING seems like a good deal when you have no deals.

And so I began with this same feeling of desperation. Any client from any niche with any budget would do. All I needed was the validation that I was good enough for someone to actually spend money on.

My beta client (a business owner I worked for free for a week in exchange for a testimonial) was a career coach, something I had on my mind too. I thought working with her would also help me understand what the market was like so I could eventually move to becoming a coach.

Thankfully working with her was a breeze. She respected my working hours, never gave me more work than I could handle and wasn't very critical of my work.

I managed to convert her to a paid client by the end of the week. But the problem was, I didn't know how. I didn't know what to charge as a beginner and hence went on to make a huge mistake of charging by the hour.

I charged her 500INR per hour. Seems like a decent amount for a beginner right?
But in that time, I would manage to create 3 carousels and a couple of YouTube thumbnails. Well worth it for her!

Now that I've learnt that charging by the hour is the worst, I'd like to share with you why.

Both you, and I unfortunately or fortunately have 24hrs in the day, nothing more nor less.

Out of these hours, say you work for even 16hrs. (Here, I'm simply taking an extreme case for workaholics to show that it really does limit you.)

What you charge per hour times the number of hours (say even 16) will give you your income.
Calculate it for yourself and you'll realise that's what your time is worth.

Sure it may seem decent when starting out but eventually

as humans we crave more, we need to get better, to grow whether it's in terms of skills or income.

But charging by the hour simply means that you're limited to a particular figure and that will prevent you from being able to scale.

As for me, after I realised hourly income wasn't working for me, I proposed a package to my next lead.

Thankfully she agreed although looking back, I really do wonder what reassured her to put her blind faith. I'm sure it must have been the crazy level of confidence I showed on the discovery call.

In the beginning the project took me about 2-3hrs per day which meant 90hrs per month.
But after about 3 months, it took me only around 30mins per day which is 15hrs per month.

See the difference?
YOU deserve to be rewarded when you get more efficient. Charging by the hour will only reward the client with more work for the same price.

Now let's talk negotiation.

NEGOTIATING

Before I begin, let me just tell you that this is Greek to me!

Honestly, till date I don't get it. I won't lie and use past tense saying at one point I didn't get it. I seriously still don't.

For me, once I take into consideration the transformation I'm able to bring my clients, that's when I fix a price for my services and there's no budging.

I really didn't even know negotiating was a problem freelancers face until I started taking my 1:1 consultation calls. One of my clients mentioned it to me and I was so confused when she asked me how to negotiate with her potential clients.
I put up a poll about the same the next day and turns out, a lot of you seem to struggle with bargaining too.

Today, I hope with my whole heart that it changes for you.

Please please don't EVER feel like you have to lower the worth of your services just cause it's too heavy on someone's pocket.
If you know for a fact that it can bring people the transformation you're promising, then there's absolutely no need to go down. You've just got to keep reaching out to people until you find the few that align with you.

That being said, I'm not going to sugarcoat it all and tell you to charge high right from the beginning. You need to first make sure you're bringing clients results.
It doesn't have to be massive, just decent.

Somewhere along my journey in the first 4-5 months, I realized that I wasn't really providing quality work. These were the words of one of my clients at the time, "Sorry but I'm not shelling out XYZ amount for sloppy work like this."

After that comment, when she called me out, I knew something had to change. I knew I had to have systems in place and have my head on my shoulders. I couldn't afford to have spelling mistakes and grammatical errors.

Even though I was charging low, I felt guilty about taking any money at all. But when I moved things around and started getting serious with monitoring minor details, I attracted way better clients. My conscience was clear and so I was able to charge high with confidence.

This is what I want for you. I'm never the one to tell you to raise your prices just like that. You can't compare your prices to those who have been in the game for years and have systems in place.

The primary focus should be on upskilling, working on yourself and getting better results each day. The confidence to then raise your prices will come automatically.

Let's take a look at a simple example of malls vs street stalls.
None of us would ever even consider going to FabIndia,

and asking for a discount when there's none stated anywhere. Yet, when we go to buy something like tender coconut or even fruits/fish on the roadside, we immediately ask for less and walk away if they don't budge.

Now the decision lies in your hands. Are you going to rise to the level of a mall or stay a street vendor and keep complaining that people ask for less?

How to accept international payments
My advice? DO NOT use PayPal. I lost 3000INR from 18000INR for no reason at all. PayPal cuts off terribly large sums of money. Not just that, it takes days to arrive, sometimes even over a month. Two of the times I received money, it took 28 days each.

The best in my opinion is TransferWise. It doesn't cut a penny from your end and arrives in a few days max, in fact mine arrived in a matter of minutes the first time.

Another convenient way is to ask the client to send through Western Union directly to your bank account. One of my clients does that to this day and I receive the amount in a matter of seconds with no amount deducted.

There you go! Accepting payments doesn't have to be that hard but yes, I do get that sometimes some apps can be a real pain.

But let's shift the focus from what's not in our hands to what actually is, what say?

Let's look at how you can create a kickass proposal that's irresistible to clients.

How To Draft A Highly Converting Proposal

"Carrie, how do I create a highly converting proposal?"

I think I've received at least 50 DMs asking this very question.

And I get it, I've been there. From knowing absolutely nothing to converting more than 80% clients after sending out my proposal, this chapter has EVERYTHING I've learnt in the process.

Let's start with my favourite part, which is Offer Stacking.

Basically, what we try to do is show the value of each part of the service and total it to see what it would amount to. We then give them a heavy discount and make it look like a deal they cannot afford to miss out on.

Trust me this works like magic!

So, here's what you've got to do.
First put down the approximate market value of each service.

Now don't worry about the exact price, to be honest, I don't even believe in market value anymore. I know people who charge 2000$ for the same service that some people charge 20$ for. No kidding!

So, put down an approximate.
(Next Page)

Here's what a sample proposal looks like-

Created for a fitness coach

Samples of graphics :

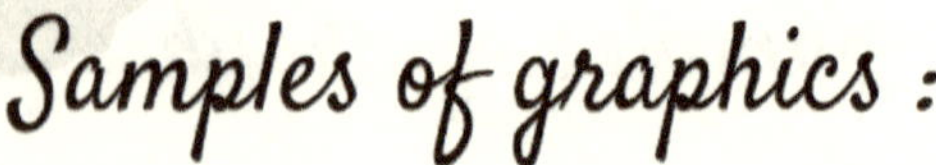

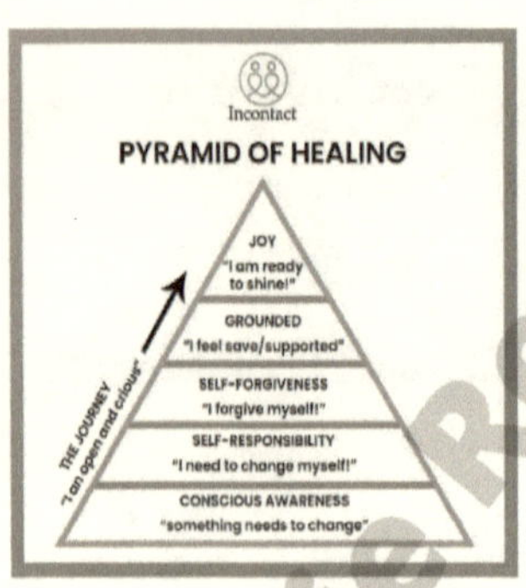

Created for a counselling firm

Samples of graphics :

Created for a life coach

Samples of captions :

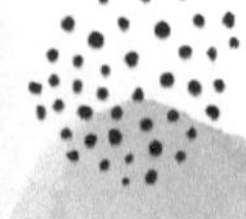

Liked by **akshayasaraf** and **23 others**

uzmanaqvicoach The capacity to feel joy is a gift we all possess.

You only need hear a baby laugh to know that the ability to be joyful is a natural and innate thing.

But, life being life, we all inevitably go through periods where we can lose touch with it, or worse, feel like we've forgotten how to feel joyful at all.

Suffering is not something we can avoid as humans.

But, how we respond to it and how we heal from it, can dramatically alter our perception of suffering, which can radically change our whole lives.

It is possible for suffering to become a pathway to a much MORE joyful life.

Do you agree?
Let me know your thoughts in the comments below

Samples of captions :

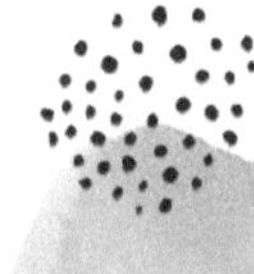

Liked by **akshayasaraf** and **19 others**
uzmanaqvicoach Admit it!

The very first thing you do the second you wake up is check your phone.

Most of us have been there, most of us are guilty.

But perhaps it's time to reflect on the little habits like these that make the biggest difference.

Like they say, the secret to success lies in your daily routine.

Are you ready to take back the power?

Are you ready to STOP giving strangers the most important part of your day?

To know exactly how you can stop these negative patterns, join day 1 of our FREE Queen of Confidence workshop.

Comment below with 'Queen' so we can send you the registration link and join our Facebook for all the awesome updates.
(Link in bio)

Samples of captions :

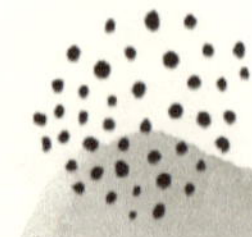

Liked by **theonetheycallvibes** and **37 others**

akshayasaraf The truth is no one, absolutely NO ONE knows what the future holds

But we can't allow ourselves to be overcome by the fear of uncertainty

Change is inevitable!

And the people who are widely successful,

The groud breaking scientists who have made our lives more convenient,

are change SEEKERS

So how about we start embracing change

How about we look at it as a stepping stone to something better?

Are you ready to change your perception of change?

Samples of feed layouts :

Samples of feed layouts :

Samples of feed layouts :

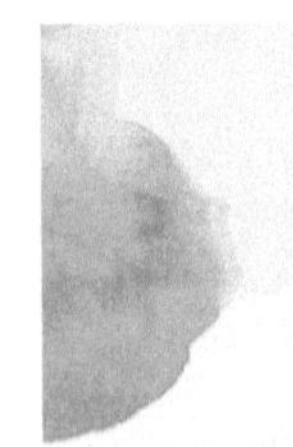

DELIVERABLES

Package 1

1) 4 reels per month ie. 1 per week (this includes sending trending audio, scripts, captions and hashtags)
Value: 2400INR

2) 4 carousels per month i.e. 1 per week (with research, designing according to brand colour palette, scheduling according to peak time) with 2 free edits each
Value:2400 INR

3) 4 static posts per month i.e. 1 per week
Value: 2000 INR

4) 15 story prompts+ Editing each per month
Value: 4000INR

5) Hashtag research (hashtag bank of 30*2)
Value: 800INR

6) Content plan with content buckets, prompts
Value: 5000INR

7) Bi weekly insight report
Value: 3000INR

(Turnover time: 48hrs)

Total value- 19,600INR

Offer Price:15,000INR/month

DELIVERABLES

Package 2

1) 6 reels per month ie. 2 per week (this includes sending trending audio, scripts, captions and hashtags)
Value: 3600INR

2) 4 carousels per month i.e. 2 per week (with research, designing according to brand colour palette, scheduling according to peak time) with 2 free edits each
Value:2400 INR

3) 8 static posts per month i.e. 2 per week
Value: 4000 INR

4) 25 story prompts+ Editing each per month
Value: 6,500INR

5) Hashtag research (hashtag bank of 30*4)
Value: 1600INR

6) Content plan with content buckets, prompts
Value: 5000INR

7) Bi weekly insight report
Value: 3000INR

(Turnover time: 48hrs)

Total value- 26,100INR

Offer Price:20,000INR/month

DELIVERABLES

Package 3

**1) 8 reels per month ie. 2 per week (this includes sending trending audio, scripts, captions and hashtags)
Value: 4800INR**

**2) 8 carousels per month i.e. 2 per week (with research, designing according to brand colour palette, scheduling according to peak time) with 2 free edits each
Value:4800 INR**

**3) 8 static posts per month i.e. 2 per week
Value: 4000 INR**

**4) 30 story prompts+ Editing each per month
Value: 7,500INR**

**5) Hashtag research (hashtag bank of 30°4)
Value: 1600INR**

**6) Content plan with content buckets, prompts
Value: 5000INR**

**7) Bi weekly insight report
Value: 3000INR**

(Turnover time: 48hrs)

Total value- 30,700INR

Offer Price:25,000INR/month

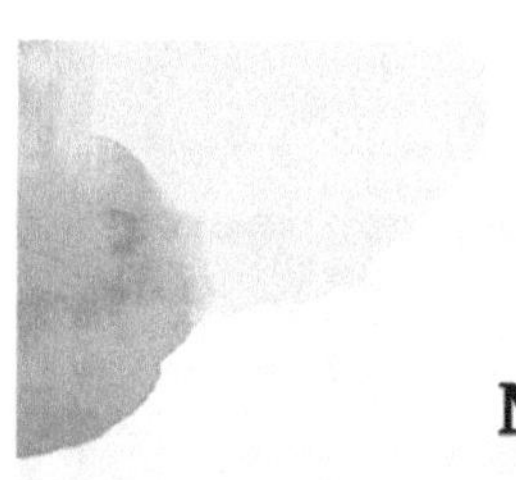

Next steps:

Once the proposal is accepted, a contract will need to be signed by both parties.

I will then send invoices as per the payment plan and package decided on which will need to be settled before any work can begin.

Once the payment is done, we will schedule a strategy call to discuss the project.

If you look closely at the page stating all the deliverables, you can see that after listing out all the prices and total value, you've got to then strike it off and put down the offer price. Do this for 3 different packages.

The idea is to make the client believe they have a choice in the matter.

Now let's move to a concept called Anchoring. This is a marketing strategy where you have three different prices in a way that the second one is ideal and most desirable.

How you do this is by under-serving in the first package and over-delivering in the 3rd.

During the discovery call, pay careful attention and list out every single need the client expresses. The second package should contain all of this. The first should have some things missing and the third should have a few extra services that you think they could benefit from.

If a client opts for the third, what better can you ask for! But the first should be a no-no. So price the first one very close to the second. This way the client will feel like opting for the second since it's only a little more than the first BUT has everything they need. The third one should have a little bit more of a margin. However, this is optional. If the second package already has too many deliverables and you won't be able to keep up with much more, then just add a few extra things and bump up the price a little.

You've got to adjust with each client, I definitely won't say any of these methods are the only way to go. Judge as per the situation and with experience, you'll have a better sense of understanding for sure.

Now, moving to all the other details that you've got to include in your proposal:

1. Duration of the project- specify the exact dates, not just the number of months.
2. Payment terms- Dates, method, amount upfront(always take at least 50% before and 5-%mid-month)
3. Next steps- what's the exact procedure they will need to go through after the proposal is accepted. Keep it simple.

Now, when you send out your email with the proposal, make sure you create some sort of urgency to let them know that they could lose out on the opportunity.

Here's what I generally say- "Hey ____ here's my proposal for your business. Looking forward to hear from you soon. Please note that these prices are valid only for a span of 5 days after which they will change based on my availability. Best regards."

As for your contract, there are a tonne of places that you can get ready-made contracts from. All you have to do is edit your name and that of your clients. If you don't have one yet, email me at carriedeannarodrigues@gmail.com and I'll be sure to send it to you.

Now for the part where they send the confirmation and payment.

This is what you're on boarding email should more or less look like-

"Hey _______

Super excited to get started on our journey together!

Let's get straight to it, shall we?

Here's what I need from you:

1. Your IDs and passwords to all the platforms I'll be handling.
2. You're branded photoshoot pictures.
3. Your brand kit that includes brand fonts and colours.
4. Any links of interviews you've given or any content you've written for websites that I can repurpose.
5. Your work hours for when I need to schedule strategy sessions or bi-weekly reviews.

I'm also attaching my 'How I work' document to avoid any confusion of work hours from both ends.

Cheers,
Your name."

If you're wondering what a 'How I work' document is, I've covered it in the chapter that talks about setting boundaries with clients.

And there you go! You just learnt everything you need to know in order to kickstart your journey with a new client and set out on the right foot.

Let's move to the next chapter where we finally take a look at how exactly you can get your first client. Note that this isn't the same as getting your next client. As a beginner, the strategies you use to land a client are very different.

HOW TO GET YOUR FIRST CLIENT

Would you hire you?

No, seriously think about it. Do you have the skills you would have looked for, as a person in the position to hire?

Your first step when looking for a client is to sit down, think about what all YOU would look for when hiring a Social Media Manager. Far too often, freelancers are so focused on client acquisition and charging their worth, that they forget to increase the value of their worth to a level that they would hire themselves, no questions asked. It ought to be a no-brainer.

The second step is to simply make up your mind!

You have to decide whether you're ready to offer your services for free in exchange for a testimonial or you'd like to charge a small amount.

It's super important to be clear about what exactly it is that you want the outcome to be.

Now, before we dive into the client acquisition process, I have to mention that I believe it's super important to be honest with clients at all times. Don't fool the client into believing that you have prior experience when you don't. Be honest, and let them know that this is your first time. In fact, some people like hiring newbies because their hunger for success and drive is more than those well settled in the industry.

Not just when it's your first client ever but even when it's your first client in that particular niche, be honest. So far, I have worked with clients from different industries so every time, it was new to me but never once did I trick them into believing anything but the truth. They were very patient with me, especially the life coach that I worked with.

Although, once I did get an enquiry to handle a makeup artist's page. She kept insisting that she wanted to see samples and I did send her all my previous work with service-based entrepreneurs but she wasn't satisfied. I didn't bother lying. I told her that I was ready to put in the extra effort to do my research to make up for the fact that I didn't have experience in the fashion industry at the time but she stopped responding then on, so yes, I've faced a bunch of rejections too. But one thing I always made sure was that I cleared the air before the discovery call, so neither of us had to waste any time.

Now, moving to how you can get your first client.

I won't lie. There isn't any sure-shot way. Some people land their clients on Facebook groups pretty easily while others find cold emailing effective. It varies from person to person. All methods work if done right, so my sound advice would be if you have a particular preference, find someone who has landed clients using that method and book a consultation call with them or slide into their DMs. Make sure you consume their free content too.

Here, I will simply tell you how I landed my first few, in case you want to model on the same.

I learnt Social Media Management from Hustle Post Academy and landed my first client from their group itself. I first offered free services and then converted it to pay. The second was through an agency, this was easy work since it was my friend's brother. The third and my first international was inbound on Instagram, after I posted a promotional reel. There you go!

Let's look at 3 reasons why you may be having trouble landing clients:

1. You aren't showing them the value of your services in terms of their business growth.
    This one definitely sounds harsh but it had to be said.
2. You don't have enough references. Referrals can honestly be the bread and butter of your business as a service based entrepreneur so never miss the opportunity to ask your clients for at least 2-3 referrals.
3. Your potential clients find your prices too high. The solution to this isn't to decrease your prices. You will have to pose the right questions by asking them what exactly it is they expect and at what price point.

What I get asked by my Indian Social Media Manager friends across the globe is "How do I get American clients?"

So this section is for you guys!

While it's a pleasure to work with clients anywhere, there's something special about Americans. They're kind at heart, very understanding and I have to say it- They pay well! At the end of the day, we're running a business and profits do matter, even if it isn't your number 1 priority.

So, how do we secure these well- paying clients then?

1. In order to understand them better, first make it a point to listen to them often.
Watch their YouTube videos and listen to their podcasts frequently. One of my favourites is Milana Saranac. When you begin to understand their mindset and references, it's easier to pitch and more likely to convert.

2. Try and use their contractions when talking to them and be free, don't hold back. Energy makes a world of difference. Many of us tend to think that Americans view us as inferior to them but that's far from the truth. They don't think we're incompetent. Our energy speaks for itself. If you present yourself confidently and showcase what's unique that you bring to the table, they will be happy to hire you. Take it from me, I've secured my fair share of clients and so have a ton of my friends who

showed up confidently on their discovery calls.

3. Don't change your accent. You may need to switch up some pronunciations here and there but you definitely don't want to seem like a wannabe or a suck-up.
People need to see their authentic self-right in the beginning. Sooner or later they will find out, so it's best to be transparent right in the beginning about who you are, what your values are, what your stand is on particular topics and what all you're willing to compromise on. Do not change anything that comes naturally to you. Use your normal accent. Of course, if there are words here and there that they do not seem to understand, make sure to repeat or write them down.

Remember, at the end of the day, you've got to be who you want to attract. Be an open minded, kind business person and you'll attract like minded individuals, who you'll definitely love working with.

It's finally time to look at what you were patiently (I hope) waiting for all this while. Turn the page to learn how exactly you can land high paying clients.

How to get high paying clients
I think from the day I stepped foot into the industry, this has been THE MOST commonly asked question.

But trust me, after reading this chapter, you'll never have that question again.

I'm going to spill it ALL out!

No more running around, trying to figure out the secrets from all the social media managers who have got international clients before.

You have me right here giving you all the ways that I land international clients.

"Okay enough with the hype Carrie, now SPILL IT"

Haha, not so fast! First, what you need is a change in approach. You've got to ask yourself "What kind of clients am I ready to serve?"

We all want high paying clients but are we ready to bring in results worthy of that kind of pay?
Trust me, even if you get a high paying client, if you aren't able to deliver results, the money won't bring you the kind of satisfaction you're hoping it will.

Far, too many people focus on getting clients. But when you focus on getting better for clients, your expertise and confidence when you show up will attract the right ones.

Now, when you do believe that you're ready, here's what you can do:

Method 1: Hang out where your ideal client is hanging out.

If you've been in the online space for a while, you definitely have heard this.

I heard it too but what does that even mean??

I don't know about you but when I hear that, I immediately think of offline conferences and events that business owners go to.

Thankfully that's NOT all that it means.

We definitely aren't going to travel to Australia and Canada just to attend conferences right?

If you're rich enough to afford that when starting out, then lucky you.

When I started, I was studying so I couldn't even afford to go to Mumbai. LOL.

Anyway, going back to what it means.

You basically have to:
1. Look for the Facebook groups they are in and join those Eg: Entrepreneurs who rule, Boss babes, etc.
2. You need to search for hashtags they use and engage with those, plus use some of those hashtags to help them engage with you too.
3. Join LinkedIn groups that they are part of.

Instead, the biggest mistake social media managers make is joining groups with other freelancers.

Yes, that's great for support initially but definitely don't have any hopes of getting hired and keep reminding yourself not to compare yourself with them. Keep going back to chapter 1 every time you are tempted to.

Method 2, and my personal favourite is reaching out on Instagram. No, I don't mean cold DMs because I'm not a huge fan but I'm not entirely against it either, since I've had a few close friends who tried it and did convert clients.

But I personally believe in building strong connections with people, so I do the same with potential clients as well. You've got to make sure to reply to their stories, start a conversation, genuinely compliment them and slowly invite them to a free call where you can provide value, help them out with anything they're struggling with and then pitch at the end.

Method 3: Cold Emailing

Gosh, it scares me!

The thought of a huge business owner taking the time to read an email that I've sent over, oh my goodness.

It has to be perfect. It just has to, doesn't it?

If you're someone who thinks like me, I'm here to bust that myth for you, something I wish someone did for me way earlier on.

Perfection is a buzz-kill. It really is.
People relate to you and feel like they truly know you only when you show them that you have flaws just like the ones they are insecure about.

That's when they feel accepted, they feel like they belong.

You do not impress with perfection. You impress by being authentic and owning who you are and what stage you're in.

So here's how you can overcome your fear and write emails that are good enough to get your call time slots booked.

Firstly, remember that when sending out emails to potential international clients, you do not in any way need to feel intimidated. Their accent may lead you into thinking they're in some way superior when in fact they are the kindest, most down to earth people who treat you as their equal and want you on their side when they hire you in their team.

Now that we have that out of the way, let's get down to writing, so we can send out some super awesome emails to your dream clients.

But but but....
Before you begin to pen down your email, you've first got to ask yourself one thing. Just one thing I promise:
What kind of pitch YOU would jump for?
What would you like the person to cover in order to make sure they aren't boring you, with unnecessary details but also not leaving out anything that you have to keep going back and forth about?

When you know you're excited about receiving a similar email, you'll also be excited about sending one out and awaiting the response.

Now, a few pointers to keep in mind when writing a good email:

1. Keep it short- Tell them exactly how you can help them increase their revenue/help their business grow.

2. Start with a hook - This is normally a compliment. Make sure it's genuine cause trust me, most people can see right through if it's just for flattery. Also, wherever possible try using their name. Makes it more personal.

3. . Use some kind of metrics if possible like how many followers you've been able to help your previous client grow to.

4. End with a CTA. Here again, keep it simple. Something like "Wanna discuss more?" or even just "Let's talk?" is good to go. My favourite one that I use all the time is "Let me know if I can send over a few time slots to chat".

But Carrie, how can I find Email IDs to send these emails to?

'Findthatemail' is where you can look for potential client's' email IDs, you really want to pitch to.

What you need to enter here is their name and company name.

However, when sending out the email, it's best that you add the website as well so it looks like you've really done your thorough research.

Pro tip: Don't ever send emails to more than one person per company no matter how bad you want to work with them.

If they discuss it with one another, it's likely that you will come off as spammy or desperate.

Now that you know how to land high paying clients, you can easily hit all your income goals. But let's look at how you can plan it all out. If you fail to plan, you basically plan to fail.

Hitting your income goals as a freelancer
Six-figure freelancer!"
Right now, this hitting that six-figure mark is being glamorized to the point that people are willing to give up their peace of mind just to earn an extra buck which more often than not, they don't even need.

When I started, I'm going to be very honest, my main goal was to hit six figures. I just kept getting on discovery calls and wouldn't even consider saying no to clients. I couldn't wrap my head around declining opportunities. In my head, I was just like why say no to an extra fifteen thousand? One step closer to hitting six figures right?

But it all came to me at the cost of my academics. I had my first mid- term when my client had a launch and as a result of the hours spent in working for her, I fared terribly thus causing a lot of stress for my finals. It just wasn't worth it. I don't have a lot of regrets but this is one thing I wish I could go back and change.

NOTHING and I mean nothing at all is worth giving up

your peace of mind for. So while I'm talking about ways to get ahead in the industry and hit all the goals you set for yourself, you've got to keep in mind that to hit those goals, you need better clients not more clients.

Taking into consideration the hours you have to spend on freelancing, divide it into the hours needed per client on an average. Based on that,you know how many clients you can take up per month.

Personally, I don't take up more than three as of now since I'm still not at a point where I'm freelancing full time. How I decided on this number was I calculated the time I could put in daily towards my side hustle. It's about 4hrs. I know that each client takes me about 45mins to an hour regularly and sometimes more when there are client meetings,etc. To add to that, I also need to devote time to my 1:1 consultation clients and content for my own pages(the 2 that I keep active as of now). So 3 clients is safe to take on. Anything more is stressful.

So say you're willing to put in 6hrs daily and each client takes you an hour, I'd say take on 5 so you can put in extra work here and there sometimes for some clients to keep them happy thus improving your retention (i.e. keeping your clients longer).

Now, how do you hit your income goals then? First set a realistic goal and one that you really need. We can all set big goals. Why not 50L per month? But we have to set something that Firstly doesn't scare us and secondly doesn't take us to a place that we're too comfortable in cause then there's less chance of growth. Say you set a goal of 1L per month and you're taking on 5 clients. The math is simple. Each client has to bring in 20k or more.

Now, one thing to keep in mind is once you secure clients or a certain level, don't go back to working for lower paying clients. You'll only end up being resentful. Say two clients pay you 25k each, taking up another that pays 15k for the same deliverables doesn't make sense. As simple as this sounds, this is something I neglected in the beginning. I took up an Indian client for 15k who needed 30 posts per month. This was after securing my 30k client for 20 posts per month.
It drained me, and I wasn't able to hire a designer or copywriter cause of the low budget. In the end, I gave up the client. If only someone had told me this when I started out!

Next let's look at how you can smoothly onboard new clients.

ONBOARDING PROCESS DONE RIGHT

Discovery call

Your discovery calls will never be the same again!

Before the call: Here's when you need to go through, do your homework. Or maybe I should just call it stalking every page, every account, every profile linked to the brand must be scrutinized. You've got to understand the brand voice and the values they stand for.

Note down anything you think they can improve on, perhaps most niche specific hashtags or location based, maybe better content pillars. Maybe they need more testimonials, etc. The checklist is as follows.

1. Check their Instagram account.
2. Look at their Facebook presence.
3. Enquire about their activity on LinkedIn.
4. Ask if Twitter is the priority for them.
5. Note down some pointers.

6. Have the floor ready on how you want to present your ideas.

Lastly, the Power Pose. This is something that has helped me gain confidence and go on to calls knowing that I am the expert. You can start doing this as well, it's simple. Stand up straight with your chest out, confident as ever. Make sure that both your hands are on your hips and stand firm, reciting in the mirror that you are capable and you are going to ace your discovery call with them. As simple as it sounds, this will give you a whole lot of confidence to go onto the call as an expert.

Before I even move to the important elements of a call, you know, I'm a huge advocate for showing up confidently, don't you? So this is a reminder that no matter how intimidating it can be, you have got to show up believing you are the expert who now has a solution to their problem.

That being said, we will now look at my signature CSECC discovery call framework:

1. Compliment: Begin the call with a greeting and a genuine compliment about their page.
2. Summarize: Then move on to giving a short summary of your understanding of their brand so they know that you have put in the effort to do your research.
3. Elaborate: Ask them to elaborate on whether or not you have missed anything and to give you a deeper insight of what their brand truly stands for.

4. Confirm: After they elaborate, repeat what they said in brief so as to confirm their expectations from you.
5. Clarity: Once all of that is finalized, ask them if they have any further doubts. Then wait to see whether or not they ask for your proposal.

If they don't ask for your proposal, then you've got to ask them if there are any further queries that you can answer. Ask if they're confused about how exactly you will help them in their business moving forward so that you can break things down to help them understand your role better.

When they have clarity, they will almost certainly ask for the proposal.

After they ask for the proposal, make sure that you let them know that you will provide different packages so that they feel that they have a choice in the matter. You can then exit the call. Make sure not to exceed over 20 to 30 minutes. It's best to keep it short and sweet and just have a sort of brief before you dive into the deeper strategies and all of which you will discuss in the first call after the payment.

No strategy should ever be revealed on the discovery call. You are an expert and you deserve to be paid for every sort of advice or consultation you may give a potential client.

Yes, I know we love to show our expertise, and we love to help as much as possible. But I made this mistake when starting out and it ended up extending the on boarding process because the clients kept wondering whether or not they should just implement whatever I've already told them instead of hiring me and asking me to do the same.

But when I started keeping the Discovery call short and sweet and letting them know that they will get all the value in the first call after the payment, they would complete the payment soon so that they could jump on that call and we could discuss the juicy strategies I have pumped them up for.

Some additional tips:
1. Get to know them better, joke a little, and keep it casual.
2. Then ask them what their business is all about, the vision.
3. Find out what their goals are for that month and for 3 months from now.
4. Ask them the current systems they follow.
5. Find out if they have hired anyone before and if so, what the experience was like.
6. Don't directly shoot but ask politely what their budget looks like.
7. Take notes all through, possibly even record the call.
8. Ask open ended questions to get them to say yes several times.
9. Use more of the words "You" and "Yours" and less of the words "Me" and "I".
10. Give them teasers like "You won't believe the amazing strategies I'm thinking of right now, super excited to get started."

11. End with action steps. I will send you a proposal in the next 24hrs. When will it be possible for you to revert?

Now we'll look at the types of clients you'll get on discovery calls and the varied approach for each:

1. Know it All- These clients are those that dominate on the discovery call. They know or they think they know what they want for their brand and how to create content for it.

So, while you won't have to put in much effort to research and pitch, you'll have to speak to them very tactfully. Never dismiss any of their ideas. Hear them out, let them do most of the talking and then if you have any inputs, you can let them know when they stop talking and give you a chance to speak but never interrupt them and barge in.

If you disagree with their approach don't tell them directly, instead suggest what you can do differently by starting with "I totally understand your point of view. Now, this is where I stand ..."

Although, I have to say, most often, these clients have good ideas so make sure to hear them out, take everything into consideration though you are the expert. Put your ego aside and pay heed to everything they say.

2. Unaware- These are the kind of clients who haven't ever hired team members before or not an SMM at least.

They don't really know what your role is exactly, how you can benefit them so you've got to lay it out in a way that they want to get started right after the call!

Like the saying goes, 'Ignorance is bliss'. It definitely holds true in this case. The ignorance of the client is your bliss because it makes it so much easier to convince someone with a fresh mind who has no biases.

With clients in this category, you've got to get them excited about the process and help them visualize the results after working with you. No, I'm not saying give them unrealistic ideas cause they won't stick with you long term that way.

Instead, paint them a picture that you know is achievable. Ask them their goals, dreams and figure out what their deep rooted desires are. For some clients it's hitting a certain income, for others it's a certain number of sales and then there are others who just want an increase in followers. So ask questions in a way that helps you understand their goal and then help them visualize themselves hitting the target with you to help.

Don't forget to give them a brief of your role. That is, you'll be taking care of the content, designs and the posting. Sone clients need all the details so ensure that everything is being taken care of.

What I'd say is, with these clients, don't attempt to close the deal on the call. Since it's their first time, they may get overwhelmed and call it off altogether later. So give them time to make a calculated decision after the call and keep in touch with them by sending in some ideas, accounts of their competitors they can model on,etc.

They will eventually come back with the confidence to begin.

3. In between- There are some clients who know what a Social Media Manager does and the basic roles. They respect your boundaries but sometimes try and push to see, if you oblige. Make sure you don't budge, especially in the beginning. How you come across in the first few weeks will determine your relationship with the client in the long run.

With these kinds, the majority part of your discovery call has to be giving them assurance. Let them know what systems you use, your process of content creation and any other details they're confused about. Once everything is clear, try and close the deal on the call itself. Since they already have an understanding, it's more likely that they will be willing to make the investment.

Follow up:
1. Either ask them if they're ready to sign right away or let them know that you'd be happy to jump on a call if they need changes.
2. If they don't respond, send another email after 48hrs saying "Hope all well. Just checking in to see if you need anything from me"

3. Don't follow up more than 3 times. If they don't revert, let them go. They are very likely to come back in a few weeks and even if they don't, there are so many others just waiting for your services.

How to ask for referrals

Getting one international client is basically a gateway to countless others.

If they are pleased with your work, they will surely be more than happy to refer you to their other business buddies.

"But Carrie, it gets a little awkward. How do I ask? And when is the right time?"

I'm coming right to it.

The right time is roughly a month after you've worked with a client.

The templates are all ready for you.

Before you get started, make a mental note to remind yourself not to skip this step.

Asking for referrals is one of the most important steps to acquiring clients easily. It saves you hours and hours that you would otherwise have to spend on client acquisition

Not just that, it ensures that you get quality clients since they are known people to your existing ideal clients. It may seem daunting initially but that's why the templates are here for you.

Here you go…

"Hey _____ it's been such a pleasure to work with you! I've honestly loved every second.

I hope you've enjoyed every bit of it too and if there's any way I can improve, I'm open to constructive criticism.

Sending you a feedback form. Would really appreciate it if you could fill it in.

{insert link}"

After they give you their feedback, they will be in a state of gratitude. So right then, ask for a referral.

Here's your script:

"Thank you so much! I really appreciate your feedback and work on all the areas you've highlighted.

Since you've enjoyed the experience, I'd love the opportunity to work with some of your business friends as well. Do you have anyone in mind who could benefit from my services?"

If they say no, politely say "It would be great if you could think about it in your free time and put in a good word for me if anyone comes to your mind. Thank you again! You've been so kind."

There you go! It's that simple. You no longer ever have to worry about finding the right words.

I would recommend switching it up a little each time though.

A client will be more than happy to tell your friend about you if you over deliver and bring a sense of professionalism to the table. Great work ethics will take you a long way. So I hope you've carefully studied the on boarding process. If not, revisit and revise that chapter right away.

Another way to ask for referrals especially from difficult clients is to share 5-10% of your profit with them. More often than not, people look at what's in it for them. This is a great way of showing them they can benefit too.

I'll see you on the next page where we'll take a look at how you can deal with tough clients.

HOW TO DEAL WITH TOUGH CLIENTS

While I sincerely hope you are blessed with nothing but dream clients, here's for the times you aren't.

Firstly, this may be controversial but I'm not at all in favour of working with family.

More often than not, it becomes more of a favour than work and there is less professionalism while also leading you to charge low.

Also, if things don't work out, it affects the relationship between two families. It's best to avoid that right?

Friends or friends of friends on the other hand, can be great to work with.

Not because friends aren't important but because it's sort of like a test to see how good a person they are when things get tough.

And if they turn against you, it's easier to move on because you'll be glad you left back someone who was toxic.

Trust me, if you go about the right way with all my engagement tasks, you will make some of the best friends who are fellow freelancers.

You won't be bothered about the toxic ones you need to leave behind. There's a whole world of people to pick good ones from.

Moving on…

Here are some signs of tough clients:

1. Someone who doesn't respect your boundaries and work timings.

I talk more about this in the chapter on Onboarding Process where I show you how you can clearly state your timings and your correspondence platforms during your period of working together.

2. When you start feeling like you're working more than 1.5-2hrs per day for a particular client, that's a red flag.
3. Asking for too many edits.
4. No mention of what exactly they don't like in a post. Just continuous disapproval.

There are several more as well that you'll learn to gauge with experience but the point of this chapter is to help you deal.

Now firstly, it's important to remember that nothing a client says about you should change the way you view yourself. Just like we shouldn't care what other people think of us, the same goes for clients. There will be times you will face insulting comments.

At the end of the day, people want their money's worth and if they feel like there is a compromise at your end, they're going to point it out. Now, the best way forward is what I call the PRB Framework:

1. Patience- Just be patient. Even if you're generally short tempered, make sure you count from 10 to 1 backwards and find a way to stay calm.
2. Remorse- After they voice out their point of view, show remorse. Even if you don't think it's your fault, show that you don't like the fact that they're upset and will do anything to make things better.
3. Better- Ask how you can make it better. If it's a design, ask them what elements they don't like. If they have an issue with posts not being put out at the right time, ask what time they think is best, if it's the length of a caption, ask whether it should have been longer or shorter and whenever possible. Always ask for references so you can understand their expectations better and model on the samples they send across.
4. Proof- Before they get so heated that they consider revoking the contract, prove to them that you'll work as hard as you have to in order to rectify the error.

Don't waste time giving excuses and justifying why it happened. Just try and do all you can and they will be pleased with your mere effort most of the time.

Setting healthy boundaries

Isn't it understood that no one works on weekends?

Well, not really! When I started out, I didn't know how much working 7 days a week would affect me.

I was so excited to even get clients that I'd do my best to please them. Whether it was submitting a post at 1am that they assigned at 12:15am or sitting down for 4hrs on a Sunday creating a content calendar, I'd always go the extra mile.

But as time passed, it drained me. When I then decided to set boundaries, the clients started to get annoyed and expected me to lower my prices since I was putting in less work days.

If you're at the beginning stages, I urge you to set boundaries NOW!

Let your clients know your work days. It's all up to you. Even if you want to take Wednesdays off, no one can really stop you. All you've got to do is communicate it well in advance.

The best way to do this is to have a 'How I work' document at hand that you can send when on boarding a new client. This document should specify your work hours, days and systems you have in place. You can add anything else that will help the client understand your process of working better, don't neglect this, trust me.

BOULDER- Create your 'How I work' document and share it In your Instagram stories, so your clients who follow you will also have a better understanding. (Don't forget to tag me @carrie.deanna so I can repost it to celebrate you.)

Dealing with extra tasks thrown your way:
At some point, you will definitely be faced with a situation where your client throws in some extra tasks and doesn't mention anything about increment in terms of your pay.

Trust me, I've been there more times than you can count. One of my clients had a launch within the 3 months of our contract and as much as I enjoyed the process of helping her out, I wish I put my foot down and asked for a hike. Although, I must say she was really happy with all my effort and sent me about 5000INR extra when it was time to make the payment for the next month.

But, the effort the launch involved was crazy. I had to send out invites daily (and I mean like 40+40=80 DMs) to her target audience asking them if they would be interested in joining the FREE live sessions we were hosting for 5 days.

Besides that, I had to stay up until 1 am to engage with the people attending the live session (in the comments) and then send out an email with the link to the recording. As a result, I ended up answering my exams terribly that month. I wasn't able to make time to go through my subject material and didn't set any clear boundaries until months later.

I don't want this for you. I want you to always be and feel respected by your clients. No matter what they may need, if it isn't part of the list of deliverables, you need to have an open conversation with them.

First of course, you've got to check in with yourself, if you have the bandwidth to take on the extra work.

If you do, then here's a script you can use in order to have a very open, honest conversation with your client.

"Hello XYZ, this is a great idea! I definitely think we should go ahead. Will make sure to add this task to our list of deliverables so things are clear at both ends. I will also send you the updated invoice and as soon as you make the payment, I'm happy to start right away."

Now, what if you don't?
All you've got to do is be open and ask them if they can hire someone else for the same. Have an open conversation.

Another option is to hire a team member whom you can delegate the extra work to or your previous work and then you take on the additional work. But if you're hiring, you naturally need to pay the new team member and so you still have to use the script asking them for a raise.

One thing that's important to keep track of though is the amount of times this keeps happening with one particular client. If it's way too often, then have a deal with them which states that all additional work will be charged for after every 15 days. This will avoid the unnecessary work of having to update the list of deliverables as well as the invoice each time.

Ultimately, most things come down to having open conversations with your clients. It's not always what you say, it's how you say it. So, remember to count backwards from 10, calm down and approach with kindness.

Taking on multiple clients at a time

As freelancers, most often we take on multiple clients at a time. Doing this can result in one of two. Either you allow one to affect the other positively or negatively.

I've done both! At one point, I had a really difficult client who just wasn't satisfied with any content. I thought maybe she didn't like my style so I hired a copywriter and designer but she had a problem with their work too. I generally don't like giving up and as a result I missed the red flags. What I did was I tried desperately to meet her expectations by devoting most of my work hours to her account. In the bargain, my other higher paying clients' work suffered. There was a lot of disconnect and the quality dropped significantly which led her to yell at me for the first time.

That's when I decided to list the order of priority with regards to the tasks for each client and not to let the criticism of one take away my peace of mind. I'm sharing this, so that if you ever find yourself in a similar situation, you can decide in the very beginning that you aren't going to pour all your energy into client pleasing.

Now for the positive impact.
You've got to look for the loopholes and include it when you feel it suits the business model of another client as well. Allow your experience with one client to give you ideas on how to make things better for another client.

For example, if one client points out that the content on the feed is very random and seems to be all over the place, come up with a theme for each week that will help you streamline things. See how the client likes this new approach and if it works well, start including it when designing the content calendar for your other clients as well.

Early in my journey, I had trouble with feed aesthetics. Every post looked great by itself but somehow when put together, the feed looked terribly haphazard. That's when I learnt about feed layouts and created one for that client. When they seemed thrilled, I created one for all other clients at the time too and each of them were equally pleased that I went out of my way to improve the quality of posts when I wasn't even asked.

So, while I don't encourage taking on extra tasks when the client requests, I don't think anyone should hesitate to put in some extra work here and there on their own in order to give a better client experience.

Setting up systems

You have no idea the amount of live sessions, YouTube videos and even courses that I've heard this from. Every expert would recommend having systems in place.

But all it did was leave me overwhelmed. It seemed like some complicated concept of having the right tools, equipment, etc.

I wondered if it would involve a lot of money, take up a lot of time or if I would even be able to do it.

Funny thing is, I didn't even realise that I already had some systems in place and I didn't even know it.

A system is basically a process that will make completing a task way simpler and more efficient. That's precisely how I look at it.

Let me give you an example of a simple system.
For my workouts, I have days organized for each body part. Each day, I have a channel that I check for

Meditation, one for stretching and then a targeted workout. This system helps me organize my workouts and removes any ambiguity that might end up with me procrastinating.

Here's another example of how I create content for one of my clients:

1. I first sit down with the content calendar for the month. I see that I need 4 humorous, 4 philosophical, 4 educational and 4 personal.

2. Then I go to an app called Meme Generator and create 4 relatable, humorous posts.

3. Thereafter, I move to Pinterest and look for prompts for the rest.

4. I proceed to read 3 articles on each subject, type out my opinion on the same.

5. Lastly, I send it to my designer and see that she completes the designs by EOD (End of Day).

I do this twice a month and that is all. 8 posts on one day, 8 on another. Simple, and barely takes more than 2hrs each time. This is my process, a system that works well for me.

Remember, the goal is to get things done faster so you can be productive instead of busy and accomplish more by doing less.

Being a workaholic doesn't prove you're better in any way. The real pros are the ones able to get work over with at decent times and then spend time with family and build relationships that really matter.

Passive Income Ideas

You know those people that you think you don't really need but you actually need them the most?

Passive income in the long run especially when you have a family to feed is one such thing.

None of us can deny that life happens. We need to shift places at times, take vacations, get married, have kids, all of which needs a decent budget and takes up so much time that it gets difficult to earn the money actively.

This is one reason why I decided to start this book. Of course the main reason is to help you and as many people as I can across the globe, but a less important reason is so that I can focus on my other commitments when I have to without needing to worry much about where I'll get my income for the month from.

Some easy ways you can start earning passive income are:
1. EBooks
2. Printable
3. Online courses
4. Design templates
5. Exclusive memberships

These are the few that I personally think are easy and in

demand right now in the market. However, eBooks are getting a little too common and so, for yours to stand out, you do need to make sure that it has an insane amount or value.

Printable are very handy and can help a lot of people be more efficient for which they'll be grateful to you. Just make sure you add your name or logo somewhere on the corner so that it serves as a reminder just like a business card but this is even better because you're sure, it won't land in the dustbin haha.

Online courses are doing really well in the market right now. While this involves more effort than most of the other options, I have to say that it's well worth it. Self-paced courses help people learn within their own time convenience so most often, they are happy to make the purchase.
Sometimes you do need to be the point of contact especially if you can't afford to hire a team member but even that is pretty low effort.

Design templates. These are for you if you have an eye for good designs and can put together a set of editable templates, maybe even in canva. Business owners are looking to simplify things and reduce the time spent on tasks. We all know how much faster content creation can get if the templates are already designed beforehand. As a Social Media Manager, you can even sell these when off boarding a client or to clients that can't afford to hire you on a monthly basis.

Exclusive memberships can be to Facebook or WhatsApp groups where you share a whole lot of value. This is something I've done personally. It helps to start groups so you can build a community and help likeminded people support one another while you also put in your opinions from time to time or answer questions. This is difficult to build when starting from scratch but in the long run, when it grows, it's very low effort.

BOULDER-

1. Think of two ways that you start earning passive income. Strictly 2, anymore and you'll end up feeling overwhelmed.

2. Once you've narrowed it down, list out all the steps you'll have to take to make it happen. If you aren't sure, look for other people who have done similar things and slide into their DMs to ask for help.

3. Set a timeline with approximate dates as to when you plan on ticking off each step. I say approximate because I'm not someone who likes rigid plans. There needs to be some room for spontaneous ideas and additions but you do need to set goals at the same time orelse it stretches on unnecessarily.

4. Start working on one step at a time and before you know it, you'll have your passive income source(s) all set up!

Admit it! You'd love to have the word 'Author' beside your name now wouldn't you?

It would be such a great moment of pride. Your family would be so proud, more clients would want to work with you, and your existing clients will have more faith in you and perhaps even agree to increase the retainer amount they're paying you.

All of this actually starts to happen. Trust me, with the simple announcement of my book, there was so much change that it brought about in my business and I want that for you too!

So here is my journey, all the secrets and tips and tricks that I learnt along the way.

When starting out, make sure to have a simple plan for the book. Brain dump and make sure to make a mind map. After you do, organize it to create a flow that you call your contents page. Once this is done, you have a rough idea in mind of where you're headed and the process of writing is so much simpler!

Make sure to have a set time every day that you stick to. Discipline is all that matters especially in the initial stages.

Decide on a device that works best for you too. Believe it or not, a large part of this book was written on my phone first thing when I woke up in the morning since that's when I find my brain to work best.

What no one will tell you to include to your book:
1. Screenshots. While many authors will tell you to include images, screenshots of certain things can also play a huge role in making things visual thus more easily digestible.

2. Checklists. Inorder to ensure that your readers are actually able to implement what they read, break things down and spoon feed wherever possible. Checklists come in handy and also make you more memorable since they think of you everytime they use it. (Okay, maybe not everyone but often enough haha)

After you write your first draft, go over things again, change some words to make the headlines more appealing, include exciting hooks and make sure the end of each chapter has suspense that leads on to the next so that they don't get bored at any point and use tools to check for grammatical errors. You'll be surprised by the number of phrases we use on a regular basis that are actually incorrect.

Each one has their own journey of writing. Some people get stuck after the third chapter, some like me get stuck when creating graphics and visuals and some like me again can't seem to ever end chapters well nor close the book cause new ideas keep popping in.

You will face your unique hurdles but always remember,

no matter what it is, someone has gone through it before and knows how to overcome the same. So don't hesitate to reach out to them asking for help. Feel free to hit me up on Instagram at @carrie.deanna if you need my help with anything.

All the best with your writing!

ALL THINGS AGENCY

When I started off I had no clue and I mean absolutely NO CLUE how I would find my first few clients.

I joined Hustlepost Academy to learn freelancing and so their Facebook group was my go-to space to look for clients.

I came up with a list of deliverables for a week that included 4-5 posts, story prompts, hashtags, posting, etc. That was how I found my first beta client who was a career coach.

I have to say I was really fortunate to have someone who was really easy on me. She respected my work and hardly ever requested edits. But the mistake I made was not setting boundaries. I would treat every day and every hour the same. I worked until 12am some days and just as much over the weekend. I was obsessed with it. I wanted to give my best.

That's what it's like in the beginning isn't it? There's that crazy hunger for success.
But as a result, the client got used to it.
After the week got over, she turned into a paid client. I quoted 500INR per hour that she willingly agreed to although I did prefer if she opted for the packages I created.
I was too afraid to push since I didn't want to upset my first client and lose her.

With time, I was given a lot of additional tasks like YouTube thumbnails and setting up her link tree. Sometimes these would barely take me 10mins since I was used to doing them. But as a result, I ended up being underpaid.

One time I remember giving her 2 YouTube thumbnails, 3 posts and 2 stories in an hour. All of which could have been well worth 2000INR+ but all I was paid was 500INR. See what I mean?
After speaking to my mentor, I realised I had to put an end to this so I off boarded her (to off board is to end the contract with a client).

My next client was an author. Here's the interesting story about how I got her.

Over the lockdown period, I was terribly bored since I was home all day long with nothing to do. So I started attending some online courses.

In one of them, we were put into groups and had to do a project together. One of the members was really sweet and I got along well with him. After the course, we'd send each other memes for a couple of weeks and have casual conversations.

It so happened that I mentioned my new venture to him one day. I just told him what my day looked like and what I've been working on.
In all honesty, I hadn't mentioned my side hustle to any of my close friends or family. He was the first. And guess what? Next day I get a text from him saying his brother owns a digital marketing agency and has a requirement for a Social Media Manager.

I couldn't stop jumping. I mean, what are the odds?! So I sent my number and email ID along with my portfolio.
I was sceptical of course knowing I barely had any experience but I showed up with confidence nonetheless for the discovery call.

That was one of the turning points in my life.
In a span of a few days I met my first client who's an author and believe it or not, it was a deal of 30000INR per month.

This was just unbelievable. From 0 to 30000 in a day. What even?! I couldn't believe my first client itself was high ticket.

So, I gave my all. It turned into an obsession. I'd send in 8-10 designs per day for approval, work on getting every tiny detail right, learn everything I was lacking in and make sure the client was satisfied.

On seeing my work ethic, the founder of the digital marketing agency decided to give me another project. Only thing, this one paid half for the same deliverables (that too being an international client).

Since I was at a point in my life where I didn't have the responsibility of paying any bills, I decided to take it on so I could learn more and get an experience of working with a company.

Side note: NEVER DO THIS! As cliché as it sounds, you've got to charge your time's worth.

Anyway, so it started off well, the content plan was decided on and we started with the posting.
With time though, one of the members started getting a little cranky. She'd pin point every tiny detail and want changes to be made. She started sending references of big accounts that had entirely different target audiences. Moreover, she'd constantly use the phrase 'You've got to get things right, I don't have the time to overlook everything'.
This clearly showed the level of disrespect for our time. Yet another red flag.

I stuck it out in spite of it all cause yes, that's how bad I wanted to make it work.

Today, I'm in a very good place with the client and I absolutely love working with them. Now, this doesn't go to say that you ought to tolerate disrespect from clients. I'm just trying to tell you what the agency founder told me. He said "Once you let go, it becomes a habit to give up easily. And thats is the beginning of your downfall."

All that said, here are some of the pros and cons of working with an agency:

Pros:
1. Little to no effort required in acquiring clients. The agency hands them to you.
2. Constant guidance from someone who has way more experience in the industry than you do.
3. Accountability that pushes you to be consistent.
4. Difficult conversations (like increase in retainer amount and apologizing for mishaps) are handled by the agency owner.
5. You're free to still take on projects independently.

Cons:
1. You can't increase your prices on your own terms. It has to be a mutual agreement with the agency owner when the time is right.
2. You are time bound when working with other team members in the agency like the designer and client servicing executive. If you decide to go on a vacation,

you still have to ask for updates. You can't decide to work at odd hours since they won't be available.

3. Quite a bit of time is wasted keeping both parties updated since you're in contact with the client as well as the agency head.

Now, because I clearly believe that the pros outweigh the cons, I'm still working with an agency. However, with time, I may just transition if the prices and timings don't suit me.

If you ask me for my two cents, I'd say if you're starting out and are placed with the opportunity provided you are compensated fairly, JUMP FOR IT!

But with time, when you feel like you can stand on your own feet and get way better clients, have an open conversation with the agency head and move on. Nothing has to be permanent. But yes, keep an eye on the details of the contract you sign with the agency.

Scaling to an agency yourself
"Whoa Carrie, let me hit six figures first. Maybe then it'll be time to start thinking of hiring a team."

Trust me, I've had these thoughts myself too but the smart way, and more importantly, the way that will keep you happy, is if you focus on tasks you truly enjoy and delegate the rest to anyone else who maybe just starting out or may have a better understanding of the field.

I know how hard it can be to accept that you can't do it all. Delegating was probably one of the most difficult decisions I had to make back when I had 2-3 clients. But I sat myself down and came to an understanding that delegating isn't for people who are incompetent. I realized that while I may be able to do anything, I certainly couldn't do everything.

So to begin with, I decided to delegate engagement. And mind you, I had to start way before I hit six figures. As much as I love meeting and getting to know people better and of course, appreciating their content, it's not something I can do on a daily basis.

Prioritizing mental health is the key ingredient to a successful Social Media Manager who can stay consistent. If you really want to make the best out of your life, you need to find what excites you most and make it a priority. Your time is sacred. It's time you start valuing it for what it is and take off any price tag that you may think you're currently worth.

Now, that you're convinced that delegating is a good idea no matter what stage you're at, let us look at the various aspects you need to consider while hiring

BOULDER 1: Write down all the tasks you perform on a regular basis as a Social Media Manager.

BOULDER 2: Highlight the ones that you procrastinate on the most.

Ask yourself why. Is this because you find them to take up too much time or you just don't like the process at all.

If they take up too much time, break them down into small tasks and see if you can split them across the day. After you break them down perhaps you'll realise that there are some sub tasks that slow you down the most. Now you know that these are exactly what you need to delegate.

Splitting tasks may not always be the best idea. Sometimes you've got to do exactly the opposite and that is to batch them. For example: If you don't like designing posts, have standard templates that you create at once and then have one day of the week where you just put them together after you've batch written all the copy.

When you're 'in the zone' as they call it, doing similar tasks help get more done. Continuing the example, if you have one day that you allot to designing, you can get 6 posts done in 3hrs but if you do one post at a time, we both know how long it can end up taking.

Now we come to the tasks that you simply don't like doing. Find out the industry rates for the tasks. Then sit yourself down and figure out if you can spare that kind of money. Do NOT be miserly here. Whatever you spend on a good team will be well worth it in building your brand and helping you get better clients, not to mention save you a bunch of time that you'll have to spend explaining if you hire an intern. So if you can spare the money, there you go!

But if you really cannot, it's time to look for interns temporarily.

BOULDER 3: Post on all your social platforms that you're hiring and state the exact role and experience you may need them to have. Also, make sure to have a clear CTA. Preferably ask them to mail their portfolio.

When posting, list out all their roles and responsibilities so that you don't have anyone unnecessarily wasting your time. List out any conditions you have as well.

BOULDER 4: Have a guide in place for all the people you'll ever hire in that domain.

Take a look at my engagement specialist's guide:
1. Comment with something genuinely nice on the top 15 posts in the feed.
2. Comment on the top 6-8 posts on any 2-3 niche specific hashtags where my target audience hangs out.
3. Send the standard DM I give you to at least 20 people per day who have a follower base of less than 3,000 (more likely to respond, that too with humility)
4. Respond to the previous day's DMs with a genuine compliment about their posts.
5. Follow them and like at least 2-3 posts, comment if possible on at least 1.

These are tasks that all of my engagement specialists have taken care of and seen great results.

Now, a few additional tips while hiring.

1. There's nothing better than people you've been following for a while and preferably have had some conversations with. All of the people on my team

right now are people who had taken time out to talk to me in the DMs back when I was playing it solo. This ensures a level of trust right from the beginning.

2. Pay careful attention to all those who adhere to the CTA. This shows that they pay attention. For example: If you say strictly Email but they DM instead, it's not a good sign.

3. Have a contract in place and make them sign an NDA i.e. a Non-Disclosure Agreement which ensures a level of trust. They will then be clear that they can't talk about the company and what's going on inside.

4. It's best to have an interview with some of the applicants that you shortlist. No matter how good their portfolio may seem, it's important to enjoy their vibe as well.

5. I'd say hire on a trial basis for a month and then fix a long term contract. Here you can test the waters and see if they're able to keep up with your pace. At the same time, don't get annoyed too soon, some people need more time to adjust. At least a month of trial is necessary.

6. Hire on a monthly retainer instead of per project. It works better both for you and your team members as well.

STARTING YOUR OWN 1:1 CONSULTATION

"But am I ready?"

"Can I really help someone else when I'm not perfect myself?"

"What do I know? It's barely been a few months since I started"

"Is my time really valuable enough for people to actually pay me?"

We've all had these limiting beliefs, these loud thoughts sounding in our heads stopping us from reaching out to people.

But trust me, there's a whole lot of truth in the saying 'You only need to be 5 steps ahead of someone to help them."

That's right! Not 10 or 20. Just five.

But what happens when they get to step 5?

See now unless you're a table, I don't see why that should be a problem. I mean, you're moving ahead too right? By the time they get to step 5, who knows you may be at 10/12 or even 15 depending on the effort you put in.

Think of someone leading an elderly or blind person. Naturally, as you guide someone else you walk ahead of them and keep moving forward so you can continue to lead the way.

Not only is it good for the one you're leading but it's a great way of keeping yourself motivated to get better too.

That said, the next big question is, "HOW do I launch?"

Don't you worry, I got your back. Even if you don't know the first thing about a launch, by the end of this chapter, you'll be fully equipped to not just go through with it but to ensure you have a successful launch too.

Mind you, I had a successful launch by implementing only HALF of these strategies I'm about to share.

If you're dedicated and make sure to follow through with all the boulder tasks, you can be assured of a successful launch.

So first things first, you need to have a content calendar in place. Your plan should be a minimum of 2-3 posts per week and stories for 5 days a week.

All of these posts I believe should have some value or at least be relatable/entertaining. In my opinion, sharing a glimpse of the value your potential audience will get after they purchase the product or opt for your service is far more likely to get people to sign up as compared to just plain promotional posts with 'This is what I'm selling. Buy now.'

Don't get me wrong, your loyal customers will keep coming back even with simple promotional content because they know the kind of value you provide but to attract new audience, value is key!

So, create a content calendar with the kind of posts, the topics you will touch upon, have a few reels lined up with trending audios and most importantly, have a story plan in place. There are so many different ways to market a product or service, so many selling points. Once you identify the pain points that you're hitting, it will help you position yourself way better.

Now, here are some TERRIBLE MISTAKES I made during my first launch that you should avoid:

1. Not talking about my offer enough.
    For some reason, I had really high expectations from my first launch. I pictured my DMs popping with enquiries after I put up my launch stories. Without building a hype around my offer, without content leading up to the launch, I somehow thought people would jump at the chance of booking a call with me. When none of that happened the way I hoped, I thought there was something wrong with my offer. I cared too much about what people would think of me showing up consistently to sell something no one had any interest in buying. But after the first 4 days, thanks to

my assistant, I showed up anyway. I paid her to make this happen and I needed to make sure to follow through with everything she asked me to, so as to make up for the amount I was paying AND get a profit.

2. Scrutinizing every tiny thing be it on the stories/posts or the deliverables/ prices of the offer.
    I've learnt the hard way in progress over perfection and I believe that 'done' is a better status than 'perfect'. We spent 3hrs trying to create attractive stories, looking for references, improvising on the offer. But in the end, I said chuck it. I just ensured all the essential copy was in and done!
    Gosh, if only I had done that going in.

3. Overthinking about the results, I'll be able to provide.
    In spite of having a ton of AMAZING testimonials from our beta launches, why do we still doubt the fact that we're capable of bringing great results?
    Now I'm definitely not going to offer you advice on throwing self-doubt out the door because I do know the wonders it can work in terms of motivating us to stay on track. But just know that too much of it will always throw your dreams in the graveyard.

4. Stuffing too many deliverables that didn't have any connection with each other.
    I thought, more the value the better right? But that couldn't be further from the truth. Your offer should solve one specific problem. My offer was to help people with a content strategy, an engagement strategy

AND confidence in stories. So my messaging got really confusing and I couldn't hit the pain points well enough.

Now that you know all that you need to avoid, let's look at what you need to actually do.

I believe that one very important part of the launch is one kickass story sequence that you post at least 3-4 times after every 3-4 days during your open cart period. In case you aren't familiar with the term, the open cart is when you're accepting payments to purchase your product or service.

Here are the elements of a good launch story sequence:

Part 1- Is this you?
Under this, you list out all the pain points of your target audience.
Example- Do you struggle with posting consistently? Are you unable to muster up the courage to show your face on stories?

Part 2-Just imagine
Helping them visualize the transformation helps take your customer one step closer towards making the decision to buy. Show them what all they will be able to accomplish after the call with you. DO NOT deceive them, be realistic or else it will lead to disappointment which is never a good thing cause they won't ever come back.

Part 3-Introduce the offer
Declare the name (Always have a name for better recall). Try and include an image of you here, preferably something bold. The name should bring in some sort of reassurance to believe they can go through a transformation with you.

Part 4-What you will unlock in this mentorship
Now it's time to be as specific as possible. Give out everything that your offer entails. More the better. This can include a 90min call, 60min follow up call, email support for a week, content calendar, engagement schedule, etc.

Part 5- Grab these bonuses
Whether you're more comfortable with an eBook, some cheat sheets or a recorded webinar, always add something additional that they can benefit from but make sure it's low effort for you.

Part 6-What's the investment
Write down a reasonable number, strike it out and put down the offer price.

Part 7- Discount
Inorder to create urgency, put up a special discount for the first 2 or 3 people who sign up.

Landing pages:
Now, while creating landing pages aren't a must, it's always more professional to have one. Ofcourse, if it's too

overwhelming and is what's preventing you from launching, just skip it. I didn't have one for my first launch and it turned out just fine.

But if you would like to create one, keep in mind that landing pages are created to get a visitor to do one thing and one thing only so always have your goal in mind before you ever begin.

I knew absolutely NOTHING when starting out, but through my journey, here are a couple of things that I picked up-

Landing page subjects-
1. Product or service page
    Goal is to sell a product or service.
    You'll do this by sharing the benefits and the end results could either be a sale or a free trial
2. Lead generation page
    Goal is to get people's information to later send emails/ messages/ newsletters with the promise of providing value.
    You do this by putting a form on the landing page
3. E-book page
    Goal- Get people to download
    You do this by getting their contact info and send them the link via email. Add the benefits of the ebook on the page.
4. Event or webinar
    Goal-Registration whether in person or virtually
    You do this by promoting the benefits of it,duration and the associated cost if any.

5. Coming soon
    Goal- Generate leads who you can email and market to later.
    You do this by mentioning the details like date and time and mention the transformation they can expect after watching the webinar.

Landing page elements:
1. Headline with or without a sub-header- The prominent text that keys you into what the page is all about. You can't really miss it.
2. Big header image or video- Great eye catcher and provides instant focus on the subject of your landing page.
3. Prominent CTA-Every landing page has a goal and that should be conveyed very clearly through a button that stands out and makes the action clear to the customer.
4. Copy to prove point and compel action
5. Additional elements, videos, charts, images- Copy is powerful but not the only way to show your point.

    Since this is a more technical subject, I'd highly recommend getting a VA who knows their way around creating landing pages. This will help you save a bunch of your time. You can choose to either learn from them or have them onboard everytime you launch.

Let's get the technical stuff over with all at once right?

So moving to sales funnels.

Firstly, is it just me or does the term 'Sales Funnels' just make you feel like you'll have to get a whole degree to learn what it means?
I never really got it for the first few months.

Fast forward 27189172 YouTube videos by random 'marketing gurus' and I sort of got the process.

But I still wasn't clear as to how to practically use it and design one for my business.

At the time, I was into network marketing. I slowly began to understand how the model worked. We found leads on Instagram either organically (by looking for hashtags of particular places/searching for friends of friends) and through paid promotions. After we got their name and phone number, we would get on a call with them and invite them for a free live weiner. After the webinar, we would call them personally again and ask for their feedback. If they seemed excited we would pitch and ask them to purchase some products so they could be part of our group. After that they had to sell or buy a certain number of products until they got a set number of points and moved to the next level. And on and on it goes.

This whole journey from beginning to end was a funnel. I had been part of it the whole time yet had no idea.

And that's going to be the same case with you. Wanna bet?

Tell me, do you have an Instagram/LinkedIn/Facebook

profile? After you started posting about your services, you received enquiries in your DMs. You then asked them to book a call and then sent your proposal. After they accept your proposal, you send over the contract and boom. That's the end of your funnel. Of Course you can extend it further by upselling when you have more services to offer but that's basically how simple it is.

Nothing is complex at all in the online space. You've just got to simplify the process as much as possible for yourself and see what works best for you. That ends up being your funnel i.e. the process you take your client through before you convert them.

Delegating
Things no one will tell you about hiring a team:

1. It takes time (longer than you think) to get someone to truly understand your needs and brand voice.
Sometimes you spend more time teaching what to do than you'd take to actually do it but in the long run, it pays off provided you retain your team members. Hiring new people every now and then will take up too much time unnecessarily.
But of course, sometimes you're forced to. For me, I had to switch my engagement specialist when she had exams. What I did, however, to ensure things went smoothly was, asked my previous team member to explain to the new one all the tasks that daily engagement involves.

2. It will not turn out as it looks in your head. Whether it's

designing or ideation for content, you will always have certain expectations that your team member may not necessarily produce. When I hired a designer, initially the designs didn't seem attractive at all to me honestly but with time, I accepted that everyone has their own taste and as long as the client was happy, I didn't have to bother too much about tiny things like that.

However, if certain things really need to be done a certain way, what you need to do is break it down and get them to understand your agenda, the outcome you're expecting from the task and why you want it to be done that particular way. This will prevent too much experiment-tation from their side.

3. They will be inconsistent.
Somehow, human that we are, we know we ought to take breaks ourselves but when team members take a break, suddenly it seems really annoying cause we're paying them right?

How I switched this around is, when I noticed my engagement specialist wasn't as consistent as I'd hoped, I had an honest conversation with her about what hurdles she was facing. She told me that she had recently gone back home to visit her family, hence couldn't keep up with work. Of course I was a little annoyed that she didn't inform me right in the beginning but instead of taunting her, I myself gave her a break for 3 days so she could spend time with family and come back stronger, refreshed.

Not only was she shockingly overjoyed but when she came back, she brought in results that I didn't even know were possible.

Always treat them right. It never fails to bring out the best in them.

4. You sometimes end up being a coach /mentor to them, not just a client.

It's always best to try different methods with each member of the team. Explain things on call, through diagrams and through text as well. See what they respond best to and once you identify it, stick to that when explaining all things then on.

How to overcome bad days
Human as we are, we go through breakups, get sick, have emergencies to attend to etc. How does all of this affect work?

As social media managers, it's difficult to take off days when we aren't feeling our best. But it's essential to put your health first short term or else you'll be forced to waste hours tending to it long term.

As strong as you may feel right now when reading this, there will come a time when you're at your weakest so put in a bookmark to hang out on this page when that day arrives.

Personally, I believe that there are two kinds of off days. One is when you just need a break from work, your body needs you to unwind and relax for a while.

Another is when there's an unfortunate event in your life. Be it an accident, falling sick, going through a breakup, etc. etc. Anything that takes you by surprise won't really hit you as hard if you prepare for it right?

So here are some things that I do to prepare:
1. I generally have a week worth of posts prepared in advance that are ready to go out.
2. I prepare some affirmations and have a page with my favorite quotes that remind me, it's okay to be in a bad place but not okay to stay too long.
3. I spend as much time as possible with my family. Having loved ones around always makes everything so much better.
4. Practice self-care. I'm not much of a face mask kinda girl but I sure do love a hot bath, a tub of ice cream and my favourite Netflix show. One binge is enough to get me back on my feet the next day. (Unless of course it's something huge like the death of a loved one in which case it could take a while.)

If it's really bad, maybe the best would be to just get out for some open-air and travel to some place. It could even be somewhere close to home but just the change in scenery can make all the difference.

I hope you find peace in your situation no matter what the

circumstances. Never forget that you are in control of your emotions so whatever happens, you can choose to view it in a positive light and move on soon instead of dwelling too much.

NEXT LEVEL MINDSET

Do YOU know YOU?

Have you figured out how much time it takes to create one post? What about 10?

Do you know how many hours of screen time you spend in a day?

What about designs? Are you capable of aesthetically pleasing creatives?

How do you go about with your writing process?

Perhaps, these are some questions you can use to reflect on for your next boulder.

BOULDER:

Write down how long each task takes you. Be mindful of what time in the day you work best, after how long you need intervals and so on, and so forth.

Knowing yourself will help you find ways that work for you. Personally, I'm not someone who works well when bound by time.

Productivity videos on YouTube convinced me to make timetables for myself when I was younger but somehow, they never worked. This led me to believe that something was wrong with me and that I was somehow incompetent.

Only a few years ago, did I start creating flows instead of timetables and this practice turned my life around.

I now write down a checklist for each day with my preferable order for completing the tasks so there's some sort of flow.

If you're someone who struggles with sticking to a timetable, I'd highly recommend you do the same.

BOULDER:

1. Write down all the tasks you know are important AND urgent to be done for the day.
2. Arrange them in the order that works for you.
3. Star or highlight tasks that are non-negotiable.

(When I say arrange in an order that works for you, what I mean is some of us like to eat the frog early in the morning and get done with all the important tasks so the rest of the day can be way less stressful. But some others prefer first building a momentum by starting with easy, less important tasks and then somewhere midday, checking the important things off.)

I'll now leave you to complete your BOULDER TASK.

Share it on your stories and tag me at carrie.deanna, if this worked for you.

YOU DON'T DESERVE THIS MUCH!

When you stumble upon money all of a sudden, your mind is highly likely to question it. Now, that's fair if you win a lottery. But when you earn your money fair and square, even if it's a sudden income boost, your mind needs to be trained to believe you well deserve it for all the hard work you've been putting in before you saw the results.

If you don't truly believe you worked hard enough to deserve it, you will not only accept it well but work harder to climb up the ladder.

However, when it's overwhelming at first and you do nothing about it, sooner or later you'll start sabotaging your success by delaying on meeting deadlines, posting average content, etc.

This is mainly because you believe your identity to be that of a poor person with average skills.

When I got my first two clients, seeing that kind of money in my bank account scared the living hell out of me. Being a college student, I barely had many expenses.

What would I do all of a sudden with all this money? Did I really no longer have to struggle with saving enough money to buy basic requirements? What did I do to deserve all this? I've been working hard for years at school, got the best grades but nobody paid me. Why now all of a sudden?

For a couple of days, this did affect me. I had to take some time out and when I did, I made the time to reflect on what was really going on. Didn't take me too long to figure out that I couldn't believe all the years of hard work are finally paying off.

I had to get rid of the limiting belief that no matter how hard I tried, I couldn't make it big because of my background. Soon after practising affirmations, the same ones I shared with you right in the beginning and pairing it with visualisation for a couple of days, I was able to get back in the game and keep growing to create a legacy.

IT DOESN'T HAVE TO BE COMPLICATED

Somehow as humans, we tend to get bored of things that are too easy so we create problems for ourselves.

Any surprise that most rich kids struggle with substance abuse? Or that often, people who cheat often come from happy marriages?

But wait. How's this relevant to Social Media?

We know that creating standard templates will save a bunch of time in the designing process, yet we waste time constantly experimenting with different feed layouts.

We know that rambling on and on in the captions is useless cause no one really reads ALL of it if it's too long yet we rack our brain trying to write long captions each time.

We know that having all posts and files organised will save a bunch of time yet most of us have messier phones than our rooms which let's face it, is bad enough.

I don't think I need more examples to justify this point. I mean, you do get it don't you?

Recently I started working with a fashion brand. The copy was fairly simple and very basic so just to justify the amount I was charging, I ended up putting a lot of effort into writing long form captions only to have the client disapprove of them. When I scrapped it off and submitted one line captions instead (that barely took me less than half the effort and time), I got the client's approval right away.

Some things are best kept simple and least complicated.

BOULDER:

Step 1: Figure out what tasks you've been complicating for yourself. Now, I know this will be a never-ending list, so how about we just stick to the ones with regards to social media, haha.

Do you forget to name your posts in canva with your client's name and date to be scheduled for?

Do you wait until the last minute every day to create posts instead of batch creating one day of the week so you can focus on other things the rest of the time?

Do you use random hashtags because you haven't created a vault for yourself and each of your clients as well?

I've certainly been guilty of most, if not all of these and if you are too, admitting is the first step to making a positive change so congratulations on getting a step closer! I hope this BOULDER will help you overcome all these hurdles and be more efficient.

Step 2: Under each task, write down what you can do to end the cycle. Break it down into actionable steps.

Step 3: Go let your accountability partner know so (s)he can keep track of your progress.

GETTING OVER PROCRASTINATION
"What if my best still isn't good enough?"

Did you know that the number one reason we tend to procrastinate and push things further or hold back from giving our best is because at least then, we'll have an excuse to say "If only had I worked harder and implemented all the strategies, I'd definitely have 1000 more followers now."

The feeling that your best isn't good enough is terrifying so we run away from it.

I did this in school ALL THE TIME and the habit stuck with me till college. I'd always wait until the last minute to study because that way I could pacify myself by saying

"IF I had to study daily, I would definitely have scored full marks."

I'm sure there's some area of your life where you've done this too.

Today reflect on just one big question:

BOULDER:

Do I hold back from posting valuable content and showing up consistently because I'm scared that after doing it all, I still won't see the results I desire?

If the answer is yes, you need to frequently listen to podcasts that remind you to face your fears because nobody ever made it big while playing risk free.

BOULDER:

Listen to a relevant podcast today.

OVERCOMING PEOPLE WHO COME IN YOUR WAY

What if I told you that you never again have to struggle a day in your life? Initially, it might amaze you, but we both know that eventually, a smooth road tends to get boring.

So why do we look at hurdles like they are a bad thing?

Henceforth, let's start looking at every obstacle as a way to spice it up for us and make life just a little more interesting.

As strange as it may sound, this mindset shift helped me overcome all the criticism and judgment of my friends and family.

Another quote I read that stuck with me is don't take advice from anyone you wouldn't gladly switch places with. So all those internet trolls, well, you don't ever want to turn into a pathetic loser with nothing better to do than spread negativity now, do you?

When I started out, no one around me seemed to get it. In fact, to this day, my parents don't get how posting a bunch of videos and images can get me to earn this much, but that doesn't bother me at all.

I'm just super grateful that they never stopped me from taking up Social Media Management just because it didn't make sense to them.

However, I do understand that not all parents are lenient. So if you are someone who is still under your parent's roof, perhaps it's time to have an open conversation with them where you explain what your vision from your business is and why you need to get started.

Now, first, of course you've got to structure it in your head. Ask yourself the difficult questions.

Do you really believe this field is meant for you?

Do you have the bandwidth to take on clients and deliver results?

What are your expectations three months from now?

Why is this vision important to you?

When you understand your vision for yourself, it is way easier to communicate it effectively to your parents or partner or anyone in your life who plays a huge role.

As for the rest of the people, their opinions don't make much of a difference to you anyway, do they? I mean, are their opinions worth sacrificing your dreams for?

Another thing that I want to add is to stop checkmating yourself! Very often we just get in our own way don't we? We set our expectations so high in different areas that we don't even realise it's actually impossible to achieve them.

Let me tell you how this terrible habit of mine led to disappointment time after time.

So, I'm someone who when having a productive day, checks off everything AND more from a to-do list with 25 things on it already.

I somehow have a knack for creating shortcuts. But at one point I set such high goals that it was practically impossible to achieve them even if I was productive every second of the day. I wanted to meal prep but also study for a certain number of hours, then workout but also attend meetings and take piano lessons.

I'd want to spend time with my family, play with my brother, cook for them, etc. and really be present but still want to attend to all client calls that would come in at any time in the day. But this just didn't seem feasible.

So I took a break to reassess things and that's when I realised, it's not a problem with my work. I can definitely do it all. I just have to set clear boundaries, communicate what exact time slots I can take calls and focus on the now at all times.

More importantly, I had to go over my day and roughly see if there really is time to get everything done, if not I'd be content as long as I ticked off all my A tasks, preferably B as well. The C could always be done the next day and I made peace with that over time.

This is a message to you not to ever beat yourself up even after you do your best. Life is such that when you focus too much on one area, you tend to slack in another and that's perfectly okay.

Some days you do need to focus extra on work. Generally, month ends are busy since they involve creating an insight report for clients and a content plan for the next month. So try and avoid making any plans with family like picnics and long drives that don't permit you to work. Infact, don't make plans at all even if you can work because the whole purpose of a trip or day out is quality time with family and work should never interfere.

However, there are times when you just can't help it. If it's a wedding or a family gathering with your extended family that has been planned with someone else, it can be a problem. But most often these are things you know of beforehand, they aren't spontaneous plans so when something like this comes up, make sure to have things done in advance as far as possible. As for me, I keep the insights of at least half the month ready so I just have to add the rest at the end. Or I stay consistent and update it every week or alternate day.

In the end, you've always got to find what works best for you but this was just a reminder to make sure it really is working for you AND those around you as well.

I'd like to end by going back to the beginning. This is a reminder that after you define your 'why' when starting out, no matter what it is, whether financial freedom, time freedom or the freedom to work from anywhere in the world, remember to keep evaluating your goals from time to time to make sure you're actually enjoying the benefits that are the whole reason why you started.

What happens very often is freelancers get so busy and blinded by the success that they forget to enjoy the perks of it.

If all you do is sit and work from your bed, what good is the advantage of working from anywhere in the world?

If all your money goes back into your business, where's the financial freedom?

If you're working 12hrs a day (and mind you, I know a handful of industry leaders who do), then what good is time freedom?

Somewhere along the way, we tend to lose our purpose and turn into slaves of the very things we were trying to enslave.

I've been there and I want to help you avoid going too far off track so here's a reminder to take a day off every once in a while and reflect on your why. It may change over time. You may have started off with time freedom and now it may be financial freedom. There's absolutely nothing wrong with that but you've got to be honest with yourself and check if your current work-life is bringing you what you set out to look for.

ABOUT THE AUTHOR:

Carrie Rodrigues is a Social Media Manager based in Goa, India. She has worked with a number of clients across the globe from Singapore and Canada to India. These include life coaches, career coaches, faith coaches, authors, fitness instructors, counsellors and clothing brands.

She is a Mathematics graduate and with no background in business, Carrie started from scratch and found her way to the top by investing in a number of courses created by leading industry experts.

She now runs two of her own Instagram accounts one of which recently hit over 34,500 followers and the other through which she lands high paying clients.

To date, she has coached beginner Social Media Managers and continues to put out free content to help online business owners.

Check out her Instagram @carrie.deanna

—--------------------